MW01073181

DESIGN FOR KID
DIGITAL PRODUCTS FOR PLAYIN

Debra Levin Gelman

Rosenfeld Media
Brooklyn, New York

Design for Kids
Digital Products for Playing and Learning
By Debra Levin Gelman

Rosenfeld Media, LLC

457 Third Street, #4R

Brooklyn, New York

11215 USA

On the Web: www.rosenfeldmedia.com

Please send errors to: errata@rosenfeldmedia.com

Publisher: Louis Rosenfeld

Managing Editor: Marta Justak

Interior Layout Tech: Danielle Foster

Cover Design: The Heads of State

Indexer: Sharon Shock

Proofreader: Chuck Hutchinson

ISBN: 1-933820-30-6

ISBN-13: 978-1-933820-30-9

LCCN: 2014941138

Printed and bound in the United States of America

*To Samantha, without whom this book would
have been twice as long and half as good.*

And to Josh, without whom this book would not have been at all.

HOW TO USE THIS BOOK

Who Should Read This Book?

This book is for anyone interested in designing digital experiences for kids, whether it's creating a website, a game, a mobile app, or a piece of software.

You don't need to be a designer or a developer to understand this book, although it does assume some basic knowledge of design terminology.

What's in This Book?

This book is divided into three sections.

The first section, **Chapters 1, 2, and 3**, talks about why kids are fabulous, crazy, infuriating, and delightful to design for. It covers the basics of cognitive development, provides a framework for design, and draws connections between designing for kids and designing for other audiences.

Chapter 1, "Kids and Design," describes the evolution of websites for kids, from the early days of the Internet through today.

Chapter 2, "Playing and Learning," defines a framework for designing for child audiences and explains how principles we use to design for kids can be applied to adult audiences as well.

Chapter 3, "Development and Cognition," dives into the stages of children's cognitive growth and highlights key aspects of child development that are important to consider when designing for kids.

The second section, **Chapters 4–9**, provides detailed information on design patterns, principles, tools, and techniques to use with kids, as well as ways to conduct effective user research and testing.

Chapter 4, "Kids 2–4: Little People, Big Expectations," provides tips and techniques for kids ages 2–4. It focuses on designing for non-readers, using color judiciously, and creating an appropriate visual hierarchy, among other topics.

Chapter 5, "Kids 4–6: The Muddy Middle," outlines approaches for designing for 4–6-year-olds, including social design, levels of feedback, and creative exploration.

Chapter 6, "Kids 6–8: The Big Kids," talks about what you need to know when designing for 6–8-year-olds. Topics include progression and leveling up, establishing rules for play, and self-expression.

Chapter 7, "Kids 8–10: The 'Cool' Factor," covers 8–10-year-olds, and includes issues like failure, complexity, advertising, and identity.

Chapter 8, "Kids 10–12: Growing Up," discusses the nuances involved in designing for children ages 10–12, who, despite being cognitively mature, still require some special treatment when it comes to digital experiences.

Chapter 9, "Design Research," explores research techniques for kids of different ages. It includes information about recruitment, release forms, and parental involvement.

The third section, **Chapters 10 and 11**, brings all the information from the first two sections together, providing everything you need to create a great digital experience for children.

Chapter 10, "An App for All Ages," demonstrates how design patterns evolve for kids of different ages. You'll see how a basic video-viewing app designed for an audience of 2–4-year-olds progresses into a complex entertainment repository for 10–12-year-olds with playlists, favorites, and sharing.

Chapter 11, "Putting It All Together," provides information about the business aspects of designing for kids, such as making your app available for download and getting your website up and running.

Throughout the book, you'll find interviews and case studies from both kids and industry experts.

What Comes with This Book?

This book's companion website (rosenfeldmedia.com/books/ design-for-kids/) contains a blog and additional content. The book's diagrams and other illustrations are available under a Creative Commons license (when possible) for you to download and include in your own presentations. You can find these on Flickr at www.flickr. com/photos/rosenfeldmedia/sets/.

FREQUENTLY ASKED QUESTIONS

How is designing for kids different from designing for adults? How is it similar?

Similar to designing for adults, designing for kids requires a strong understanding of your users and what they need and want. However, what differentiates designing for a child audience and an adult one is that children change really quickly. In just six months, a 2-year-old experiences significant cognitive, motor, and technical growth, while an adult's skills in these areas remain pretty stable. It's important to keep these changes in mind as you develop sites and games that can grow with your audience.

Also, while adults usually have a clear end goal in mind when they use an interface, kids are in it for the journey. Just using a computer or an iPad is a treat for them. It's all part of the adventure. You'll still have requirements to follow and goals to achieve, but for the most part you can have a little more fun with the details. Chapter 2 provides more information about these similarities and differences and what they mean when designing for different audiences.

How much do I need to know about children's developmental stages in order to design for them?

It's good to have a basic understanding of where kids are developmentally when designing for them. While you don't need extensive knowledge of cognitive psychology, it makes sense to brush up on the stages of cognitive growth and maturation before starting a design project. In Chapter 3, you'll find a primer on Piaget's Stages of Cognitive Development, which will provide information about the various stages that children go through in order for you to design compelling experiences for them.

What rules and regulations do I need to be aware of when designing for children?

While there aren't hard-and-fast rules for the design of sites and apps for children, many countries have strict regulations about the collection of personal information from kids younger than 13. You can find a detailed explanation of the U.S. COPPA (Children's Online Privacy Protection Act) laws, which are among the most stringent, in my interview with Linnette Attai at the end of Chapter 6, These regulations state that parents or legal guardians must agree in writing to any information collected from kids that will be used to message them, market to them, or in any other way identify them, including any type of behavioral or geographic targeting.

In 2008, at the 30th International Conference of Data Protection and Privacy Commissioners held in Strasbourg, a Draft Resolution on Children's Online Privacy was created. These guidelines are high level, but set the stage for international agreement about protecting kids' identities online. They include a call for increased collaboration among designers, educators, parents, and kids—and the companies that create digital products for them—to ensure that all personal information is protected.

Are there specific design conventions I should follow when designing for kids?

You'll need to be aware of the unique characteristics of the specific age you're designing for and design to those characteristics. For example, when designing touch-screen apps for kids 2–4-years-old, you'll need to make sure the touch targets you create are large enough for little clumsy hands, and that the gestures you design map to behaviors kids already do, like swiping, grabbing and smacking instead of flicking, pinching, and tapping. A detailed explanation of these can be found in Chapter 4. In addition, you'll need to rethink many of the icons and symbols you use, even if they are universally understood icons for adult audiences, since kids are still learning to think abstractly. Finally, you'll need to rely less on text explanations and more on visual demonstrations, because kids—even those who can read—have a hard time scanning words on a screen. Chapters 4–8 provide details on the design patterns that are most effective for kids of different ages.

CONTENTS

CHAPTER 5

Kids 4–6: The "Muddy Middle"   71

CHAPTER 6

Kids 6–8: The Big Kids   87

FOREWORD

As a parent as well as a researcher and designer of interactive media for over 30 years, I have found the world of digital design for kids fraught with condescension, oversimplification, and downright sloppiness. Children, because they are not adults, have seemed *not* to require elegant and thoughtful design. According to many developers, designing for kids must somehow be easier because kids are simpler than adults, aren't they? All you need is a good property license like *Superman* or *ET* (as the old Atari would have it), and you're good to go.

Debra Levin Gelman has done a great service for kids in the digital world by writing this thoughtful, thorough, example-filled book for the designers of digital games and apps for children. The text itself is remarkably well informed and communicated in a straightforward manner. By including a huge variety of examples with screen shots and excellent critiques, Gelman shows as well as tells. Her case studies and interviews also enrich the reading, and they demonstrate that Gelman knows her subject thoroughly and first-hand. Each chapter addresses a particular two-year age range, tracking developmental and social features of the age group and providing a concise set of design heuristics. A final chapter on design research with children gives designers methods for reaching out to their audiences and "absorbing," as Gelman puts it, their mind-sets and preferences.

Throughout the book, specific insights caught my eye—sometimes because they matched my own experiences so well, and sometimes because they took me by surprise. In the 2 to 4 age range, for example, I was surprised and pleased to see Gelman's painstaking analysis of the successful use of visual indicators to communicate hierarchy and focus. Her examples of parents' frustrations with their kids repeating actions that would lead to certain kinds of noises were illuminating for me (although it did not change my long-held belief that things that make loud, repetitive noises are toys from hell and should probably be taken into the driveway and run over). In the 4–6 age group, I was delighted by Gelman's observation that "sometimes, making something feel social is as easy as presenting it in the first person." Having conducted many years of research on relationships between gender, technology, and play, I resonated deeply with her heuristic that the designer's response to gender should be guided by how kids play rather than who we think they are.

I am fondest of the observations and heuristics that have to do with how design may nurture the delicate development of what we may later call "critical thinking skills." For example, marking the distinction between advertising and content when a child is just beginning to be able to recognize the difference can help kids develop into adults with informed criticality of media and messaging. One of my favorites of Gelman's bits of advice is that we make younger kids' experiences of "losing" or "being wrong" more interesting. The notion of an interesting failure can lead to the kinds of criticality and bravery that make for resilient, creative adults. These qualities among others are fostered by application of Gelman's insights about design.

Although the book is crisp and clear-eyed about its subject, it reveals Gelman's love and respect for persons of a tender age. I hope that everyone who designs interactive stuff for kids will read it and take it to heart.

Brenda Laurel
Santa Cruz Mountains, California

INTRODUCTION

My interest in children's media started many years ago in college when I took a course on kids' television from the brilliant Patricia Aufderheide. A mother of young children at the time, Dr. Aufderheide combined real-world examples with principles of cognitive psychology to demonstrate how exciting, rewarding, and *difficult* it is to create meaningful media for little ones. Through her teaching, I learned about the importance of visual literacy—helping kids understand how design techniques can be used to inform, sell, manipulate, and educate—and realized that, while there were a few gems out there, most of the television programs for kids were little more than veiled product advertisements. Children's television was deregulated in the mid 1980s, and much of the high-quality kids programming developed before that time gave way to commercials disguised as animated half-hour shows.[1] My interest in the medium grew, and I envisioned myself writing for shows like *Sesame Street* and *Reading Rainbow*.

Then the Internet came along. I went to grad school. I became familiar with educational technology pioneers like Seymour Papert, Brenda Laurel, and Sherry Turkle, and got to study with the amazing Amy Bruckman. I learned that while the Internet opened all kinds of doors to better kids' media, we still had a long way to go.

I got a job designing kids' websites. I worked with brands like Crayola, Scholastic, PBS, Comcast, Campbells' Soup Company, and Pepperidge Farm. I got to work with hundreds of kids. And I got to design for kids as though they were kids, not just small adults capable of deductive reasoning, abstract thought, and logical progression.

When my daughter was about 2, I began taking a closer and more critical look at kids' media. The iPhone was a few years old at the time, and the possibility of using this device to teach and entertain was especially appealing, because it didn't require a keyboard, a mouse, or highly developed fine motor skills. I looked for tips and techniques on how to design apps for kids and found some interesting articles, but no single comprehensive resource on designing

---

1   http://www.awn.com/animationworld/dr-toon-when-reagan-met-optimus-prime

compelling digital products for children of different ages. So I put together a quick elevator pitch and approached Lou Rosenfeld. That conversation led to this book.

When I started writing this book, I intended for it to be a primer on how to design for kids. But as it began to unfold, I realized that many of the techniques we use when designing for children can also be used to design great experiences for users of all ages. I hope that this book will be of value to you and that the information you find here will help you become a better designer, regardless of whom you design for.

Debra Levin Gelman
May 13, 2014
Philadelphia, PA

CHAPTER 1

Kids and Design

Savannah W., Age 3

You can't stop the future.
You can't rewind the past.
The only way to learn the secret
...is to press play.

—Jay Asher

Thirty years ago, computers were rare, special, fragile machines that kids got to play with for a few hours a week during computer time at school. Now they are ubiquitous, gracing desktops, counters, and classrooms across the globe. Twenty years ago, children were given floppy disks and monitored closely as they learned BASIC and played games. Today, they're handed laptops and tablets and allowed to explore freely. Ten years ago, fear of the unknown had kids shying away from this thing called the World Wide Web. Now, children are boldly tackling the Web—in addition to apps, social media, and MMORPGs—with little to no fear holding them back.

This generation of kids is digitally native, meaning that technology has and always will be a part of their lives. Unlike previous generations, these digital natives believe that technology exists to serve them, instead of the other way around. They have always known "reset" and "undo" and "play again." They see technology as a tool for expression, experimentation, and communication. And designing for these little people is more challenging and more exciting than it's ever been before.

Let's take a look at what it meant to design for kids back when the Internet was a child and what it means now that the Internet is well into its adolescence.

Designing for Kids, Then...

The first children's website I ever designed was back in 1998 for Georgia Public Television. It was a companion site for a TV show called *Salsa*, which taught preschool kids basic Spanish. The website had yellow text on a dark green background, a few animated gifs, some really choppy videos, and a game that I had cobbled together in Shockwave (see Figure 1.1). The navigation was complicated, and there was way too much instructional copy. But I was proud of it, and it even won a public-television award for "Best of the Web" or something like that.

FIGURE 1.1

A screenshot from my first kids' site, circa 1998.

The show *Salsa* is still around, but the website is long gone. Back in the early days of the Web, we designed websites for kids just like we designed them for adults. The differences were that we used a lot more pictures, a lot more color, and bumped up the font size a few more points. We figured that "bigger" meant it would appeal more to children. True, we were limited by modem speeds, Web-safe colors, and smaller monitors, but, constraints aside, we didn't really challenge ourselves to think of different and better ways to approach designing websites specifically for kids.

In fact, quite the opposite was true. We were concerned with keeping kids away from the Web and protecting them from the sudden onslaught of unmoderated news, pictures, and information surging into our homes from all over the world. While "educational" sites were cropping up all over the place, the assumption was that they'd be used alongside a responsible adult who could help navigate the difficult and rocky terrain. Because kids couldn't be trusted with this crazy, scary new technology.

Sites for children have been around since the Web was in its infancy, but it's only in the past 10 years that we've seen a strong focus on designing for kids' unique cognitive, motor, technical, and emotional skills.

Figure 1.2 shows a perfect example and prototypical turn-of-the-century kids' website called *Enchanted Learning,* which was meant to be used with parent or teacher assistance. This site featured some interesting educational content for kids, but the antiquated design, overuse of color, limited grid, and tiny images made it difficult for children to understand and use. However, when the site was first created in 1996, it represented the best that we had to offer young people in terms of digital design. Those were the days before Flash, when interactivity and engagement were limited, and we assumed that all our users could read, use a mouse, and had the patience to wait for a bunch of pictures to download. Boy, were we ever wrong!

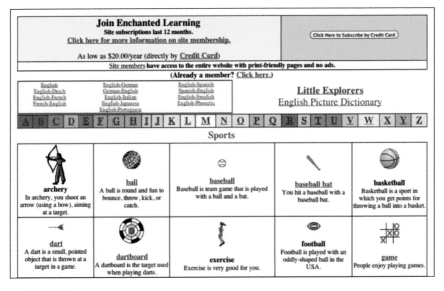

FIGURE 1.2
Enchanted Learning is a typical kids' website from the mid-1990s.

...And Now

Now, fortunately, we know better. Advances in technology, a deeper understanding of how kids use this technology, and a greater sense of comfort and trust have given us a broader toolkit with which to work and design. So the result is a renewed commitment to designing top-notch experiences for kids, as evidenced by Apple's new app-store "Kids" category, as well as exciting, cross-channel experiences that bridge the gap between the physical and the virtual. We're starting to realize that we need to maximize the time that children spend using technology so that it truly meets their cognitive, developmental, emotional, and intellectual needs. But, as you'll soon see, there is still a lot of work remaining to be done.

Just for comparison's sake between then and now, let's look at *DIY*, an example of what a great new digital experience for kids entails today.

DIY is a website (with a companion app) that is really and truly *for kids*. Its judicious use of color, its large, touchable buttons, and its straightforward navigation and flow make *DIY* a great omni-channel experience for children and their ever-evolving cognitive abilities. *DIY* enables kids to find creative projects online, which they can then create "in the real world" and go back and share with their digital community. *DIY* maps perfectly to how kids ages 6 and up like to use technology—to browse, to sort, to filter, and to support the activities they do in the real world. Younger kids have a harder time separating what they do in a physical space from what they do in a digital one, and *DIY*'s seamless cross-channel presence makes this separation all but unnecessary (see Figure 1.3).

In addition to a clear, strongly executed creative design, *DIY* uses interaction-design patterns that work perfectly for kids under 12. Straightforward flows, lots of options to choose from presented in a manageable and understandable format, and obvious navigation help kids know exactly what the site is for and how to use it. We'll look at more examples like this one throughout the book.

FIGURE 1.3

DIY is a cross-channel experience that represents the new direction in digital design for kids.

The Good and Bad News

The *good* news is that we're seeing more and more sites and apps like *DIY* that are available for kids today. The *bad* news is that we're not seeing enough of them. There are still far too many mediocre experiences for kids out there—apps, sites, games, even toys—thrown together with little to no regard for how children learn and play. As designers, we have a tremendous, untapped opportunity and responsibility to design great experiences for kids.

The Council on Communications and Media[1] reported the results of a study conducted in October 2013, which found that children in the United States average about eight hours of screen time a day, includ-

---

1 Council on Communication and Media. 2013. Children, Adolescents, and the Media, *Pediatrics* 132:958-961

ing TV, video games, websites, and mobile devices. While we're not looking to increase those hours, our goal as designers should be to improve the quality of children's apps by creating better interfaces, better experiences, better content, and better tools for them. This book is designed to help you do just that. So let's jump in and start learning about kids and design.

CHAPTER 2

Playing and Learning

Clara, Age 8

You can discover more about a person in an hour of play than in a year of conversation.

—Plato

At a 4-year-old's birthday party, I had an interesting conversation with two different parents about their children's iPad use versus their TV watching. I asked about the rules these parents had in place regarding screen time for their kids. One mother strongly objected to any "playing" on the iPad for her child. Instead, she let her son—a very intelligent, developmentally sophisticated 4-year-old—use age-appropriate reading and math apps for about an hour a day, and then allowed him to watch two TV shows before bedtime.

The other parent let her 3-year-old daughter play games and watch videos on the iPad whenever she wanted. Her favorite game was *Angry Birds*. She explained how her little girl was frustrated in the beginning because she could only launch the birds backward, but that she had finally figured out how to turn the slingshot around and launch the birds toward the targets. This mother talked about how excited her daughter was when she knocked over the pigs and was able to really "play" the game as intended. The mother also noticed significant progress in her daughter's hand-eye coordination. At the time, the other mother of the boy shook her head in disapproval, clearly disagreeing with playtime or watching videos on an iPad.

So Which Is It? Playing or Learning?

Is one of these parents right and the other wrong? Maybe. Despite a multitude of studies[1] done about kids and screen time, no one really knows what effects TV and interactive media will have on their development. What we do know, however, is that both kids described in the previous example are playing and learning. Whether they're learning reading and math through traditional teaching principles,

---

1 V. Rideout, E. Hamel, and the Kaiser Family Foundation. *The Media Family: Electronic Media in the Lives of Infants, Toddlers, Preschoolers, and Their Parents* (Menlo Park, CA: Kaiser Family Foundation, 2006).

F.J. Zimmerman and D.A. Christakis. Associations Between Content Types of Early Media Exposure and Subsequent Attentional Problems. *Pediatrics* 120, no. 5 (2007): 986-92.

or physics and hand-eye coordination through games, they're learning concepts, skills, and strategies that will ultimately serve them in life. They're also developing new schema for interpreting the world around them.

It's easy to lose sight of the fact that kids learn and communicate *through* play. As a designer, you're responsible for understanding your audience and creating experiences based on the way that people prefer to complete tasks. However, as a designer for kids, you're responsible for understanding that kids prefer to complete their tasks, such as learning, through play.

Unfortunately, education systems in many countries throughout the world have taught us that playing and learning are separate activities—one is conducted in a classroom setting, and the other on a playground. In fact, every time designers mention the importance of play when designing for kids, they usually counter it with this thought, "But I want to create something educational, to help kids learn. I don't want to make just another game."

In actuality, the most successful kids' sites and games do have learning at their core. Games like *Angry Birds* and *Where's My Water* teach complex physics principles to children as young as age 5. Sites like *Webkinz* and *Club Penguin* teach currency, philanthropy,[2] and money management. And apps such as *Toca Band* and *Baby Piano* teach the basics of music composition. The key difference between these experiences and more traditional "learning" games is that they put play front and center. The educational aspect, even though it's the primary goal, takes almost a backseat for kids as they strive to master the complex machinations of the game.

> **NOTE** THE DICTIONARY SAYS...
>
> *Merriam-Webster* defines "playing" in a number of ways including "a recreational activity, especially the spontaneous activity of children." Whereas they define "learning" as "the activity or process of gaining knowledge or skill by studying, practicing, being taught, or experiencing something."

---

2 http://massively.joystiq.com/2008/02/10/
club-penguin-kids-turn-mmo-fun-into-1-million-for-charities/

Designing for Kids vs. Designing for Adults

You now know that designing for kids is different from designing for adults. But how is it different? Actually, the differences are much more subtle and nuanced than people thought just a few years ago. When you are designing for adults—even when designing games for adults—the goal is to help them cross the finish line. When you are designing for children, the finish line is just a small part of the story. Here are some key differences to consider:

- Challenge

- Feedback

- Trust

- Change

Challenge

Kids delight in challenge and conflict, regardless of their goals. Adults, when they are trying to accomplish routine tasks like checking their account balances or reading email, don't. Toca Boca, a Swedish company that makes wonderful apps for preschool and elementary-aged kids, nails this concept with its *Toca House* iPad game (see Figure 2.1). In this game, kids have to clean a rug by swiping a vacuum cleaner over it. Instead of making the dirt disappear after a single swipe, the Toca Boca design team created a more challenging interaction, where the dirt fades slowly with each swipe. While this ongoing friction would drive adults nuts, kids love it. According to Toca Boca company cofounder Emil Ovemar, profiled at the end of Chapter 4, the added challenge makes the accomplishment more significant for kids, and also makes the app feel more exciting and fun.

Conflict is important for adults, too, but at a more macro level. Conflict in movies and in games for adult audiences helps move the story along, but for kids, little micro-conflicts, like cleaning up a dirty rug, help them resolve their own inner conflicts. LEGO did an interesting study on "conflict play" where it determined that conflict helps "…youngsters develop skills such as:

- Predicting how others are likely to react to their behavior

- Controlling their own emotions

- Communicating clearly
- Seeing other people's points of view
- Creatively resolving disagreements"[3]

FIGURE 2.1

Toca House offers the right level of "conflict" to keep kids engaged.

Feedback

Kids love visual and auditory feedback whenever they do anything in a digital space. If you open any site or app that is designed for kids, you'll see that every interaction produces some sort of response or reaction. On the other hand, adults like to get feedback at the point of success, or when they do something wrong. Unlike kids, adults tend to get annoyed when every movement of the mouse or every gesture on a mobile device results in a sound or animation. Imagine if you were trying to balance your checkbook online, and every time you entered a number or clicked the "return" key, you heard applause and saw a little animation. You'd be pretty annoyed, right? Not kids. They like to be rewarded for everything they do.

---

3 http://parents.lego.com/en-us/childdevelopment/conflict-play

Trust

Kids are much more trusting than adults, generally speaking, because they are unable to see or understand the ramifications of their actions ahead of time. Kids can be taught not to talk to strangers online or give out personal data to people they don't know, but unless something bad happens as a result, they can't fully anticipate the results of what they do online. This behavior continues through the teenage years, and it explains the risky behavior of teens both on- and offline.

In 2007, Laurence Steinberg, PhD, of Temple University, concluded that the slow maturation of the cognitive-control system, which is responsible for impulse control, could lead to risky behavior in kids between puberty and adulthood.[4] While apps like Facebook, which allow kids 13 and older to participate, don't actively encourage risk-taking, they do very little to prevent trusting children from "friending" people they don't know. As designers, you are responsible for understanding this trust issue and build safeguards to protect your young users (see Chapter 6 for more information).

Change

As anyone knows, kids change pretty quickly, so when you design for a 3-year-old, you know that the app you're designing probably won't work for a 6-year-old. Consequently this book is broken into two-year age increments, so you'll be able to understand these differences and the implications they present for design.

I was once asked to design a website for kids ages 6–11, which is a ridiculously large age range. I ended up designing levels, not to limit children's play but to allow them to access content and activities appropriate for them. It worked, but my preference would have been to focus on a much smaller age range to increase usage and appeal.

Adults, on the other hand, are generally pretty consistent in terms of cognitive capacity, so they aren't apt to change as frequently as children.

---

4 Laurence Steinberg, Risk-Taking in Adolescence: New Perspectives from Brain and Behavioral Science. *Association for Psychological Science* 16, no. 2 (2007): 55–59.

The Similarities Between Kids and Adults

Even with these differences, it's important to note that there are quite a few similarities between designing for kids and designing for adults. These include the following:

- Consistency

- Purpose

- Surprise

- Lagniappe

Consistency

When designing apps, make sure that your design patterns are consistent. Both kids and adults get annoyed by design elements that seem random and unnecessary. A common misperception about designing for kids is that they like everything on the screen to do something cool. In fact, it's quite the opposite. Children like items on a screen to do cool stuff as long as there is a method to the proverbial madness.

Elements that get in the way or animate spontaneously or don't contribute to the overall goal can frustrate kids and adults alike, and cause them to abandon a game or an app entirely. In addition, if everything on the screen moves, is brightly colored, or makes noise on the same level, kids and adults become confused about what is interactive and what isn't, and this makes it very hard for them to use the site or app. A common design principle for adults is to keep interactions and feedback consistent so that users will be able to learn how use the site or app quickly. The same is true for kids.

Purpose

Kids, like adults, need a reason to use a site or an app, and they need this reason to be evident right from the start. While kids will be more open to exploring and learning than adults, they'll get bored quickly if they are not immediately engaged in the goals and purpose.

For example, if it's a game, will it be fun? If it's a tool, what will it help them do or learn? They need to know what's in it for them before they're willing to fully engage. This doesn't necessarily mean that you have to create detailed explanations or how-to videos, but it does mean that you have to communicate clearly what your app is and how it works before users have time to decide they're not interested.

Surprise

Both kids and adults develop expectations around how a site or app will behave, and they like to have those expectations met. Neither kids nor adults are particularly interested in being surprised, or in having an experience deviate from how they expect it to work.

As an adult making a purchase online, after you submit your payment, you expect to see a message confirming your purchase, not a pop-up ad with a video trying to sell you something else. As a kid adding gems to a box in a game, you expect to be able to open the box where the gems are stored to see them all, not to have to open the box, pull out drawers, and hunt for the stuff you thought was in there.

Lagniappe

I first heard the word *lagniappe* from my editor, Marta. A lagniappe is a little something extra—an "Easter egg"—thrown in to delight users or customers, and both adults and kids enjoy these small, unexpected interactions that enhance their experience with a site or app. For example, Twitter's mobile "pull down to refresh" option shows a nice little animation, letting users know their feed is being updated. If kids leave the *Talking Carl* app open for a few minutes without interacting with it, it sings softly to itself to get their attention. It's important to note that there is a difference between a "surprise" and an "unexpected delight," however. A "surprise" is when the jack-in-the-box jumps out and scares the crap out of you. Lagniappes are the frozen grapes the hotel passes out while you're overheating by the pool.

> **NOTE** **NON-TRADITIONAL EASTER EGG**
>
> Wikipedia defines an Easter egg as an intentional inside joke, hidden message, or feature in a work such as a computer program, movie, book, or crossword. According to game designer Warren Robinett, the term was coined at Atari by personnel who were alerted to the presence of a secret message that had been hidden by Robinett in his widely distributed game, *Adventure*.

You'll want to be aware of these differences and similarities when designing for kids. Remember that designing for children isn't just a matter of taking content, images, and interactions meant for adult audiences and "dumbing them down." You'll need to make a conscious effort to understand where your users are cognitively, physically, and emotionally and make sure that your designs map to them appropriately. Conversely, if you look at designing for kids as completely different from designing for adults, you'll lose sight of some of the key conventions and patterns that are hallmarks of good digital design.

A Framework for Digital Design

While the overall process of designing for kids is similar to designing for adults, you'll still need to conduct user research, analyze your findings, design your product, and test it out. However, you'll conduct the activities in very different ways. I call this process the "4 As" of designing for kids: absorb, analyze, architect, and assess. You'll recognize a lot of the steps listed below, but the things you'll look for and the way you'll measure success are quite different.

Absorb

As a user-experience designer, you really might be tempted to open a sketchbook and start sketching ideas for the next big site or app. You have a great idea in mind, and you want to start playing around with it to see what it might look like. When you are designing for adult audiences, this may sometimes work, as you probably already have an understanding of what your audience wants and expects, but with kids, especially younger ones, you have to observe them in order to truly understand them. I've heard designers say, "I remember what it was like to be a kid, so I'm probably okay without conducting observational research, right?" or "I have kids the same age as our target audience, so I can just use what I know about them to do the design." Not the case. As explained earlier, these digital natives are much different than we were when we were kids, and they are changing constantly in terms of behaviors, needs, and expectations, so be sure you always do some level of absorbing, even if it's with a small number of children.

The first step is to spend lots of time watching kids and absorbing everything about them—how they play, communicate, manipulate objects, and interact with items in their environment. As you'll quickly discover, kids lack the deductive reasoning that adults have, and as a result, they cannot make the cognitive leap between an intangible idea and an actual interface. They are also not great at expressing themselves verbally yet. In order to understand what they want, or what makes them tick, you need to conduct observational research. And it's more than just observation, it's truly absorbing all of the rich data that children provide with everything they do and say.

Fortunately, observational research is relatively easy to conduct. You don't need an elaborate test script or a fancy lab with state-of-the art technology or a complicated recruitment screener. You need a room with a bunch of age-appropriate toys and games, or, better yet, some kids whose homes you can visit to observe them in their everyday surroundings. You do need to be clear before conducting this research on what you want to learn from the research and how you will use the data. For example, if you want to learn how 6-year-old girls approach collaborative construction activities to inform the design of a coding game, you'll need to make sure you have the appropriate objects on hand, the right number of girls participating in the research, and enough time for the kids to get to know each other and create something together.

TIP FINDING THE RIGHT PARTICIPANTS

> Along with clearly understanding what you want to learn from your absorption sessions, you'll need to make sure that you have the right participants. For example, if you're designing a game to be played on an iPad, you should observe kids who use iPads regularly. That way, you know your participants will understand the context in which your game will be used.

We'll talk a lot about actual design research in Chapter 9, but for now, the main thing to remember is to focus on observing and absorbing how kids play. Children communicate volumes simply by how they play, what they choose to play with, how long they choose to play with it, and when they decide to play with something else.

It's important to choose specific types of play that relate to the app or site you want to create. For example, if you're designing a game that lets kids make their own music, have the children show you their favorite instruments and watch how they use them. For example, younger kids will tend to bang on a toy xylophone, but older children may actually attempt to tap out a melody.

If you're designing a site about cars and trucks, give kids toy vehicles and see what they do with them. For instance, you'll probably notice that boys like to line up cars in rows or race them down ramps. Girls, on the other hand, like to assign personalities to the vehicles and have them "talk" to each other, as they would with dolls or toy animals.

You'll also want to pay special attention to how kids interact with the objects in their environment. Some kids, especially younger ones, are very "toy-oriented," meaning they prefer to play with physical objects, as opposed to inventing their own games or playing pretend. That behavior typically occurs because younger kids are still figuring out how they fit into the world around them, and they need to establish a connection to, and separation from, the objects in their space. Watch how closely kids "play by the rules"—for example, do they put the toy pilot into the cockpit of the plane and play airline, or do they turn the airplane upside down and put animals and crayons and trucks in it?

You'll probably see a mix. This will help you determine how constrained you want the rules of your site or app to be. If kids are consistently associating non-traditional behaviors to the objects you've given them, you'll want to make your app less about the objects themselves and more about all the cool things kids can do with them. If kids are staying true to the nature of the objects, you'll want to focus more on these unique attributes of the objects themselves. You'll probably notice some age discrepancy here. Nothing's more fun to a 3-year-old than doing crazy things with common objects. A 6-year-old, on the other hand, will prefer to play it safe and use the object as intended.

Analyze

Now that you've done all this observation, you'll need to figure out what it all means for your content and design. I tend to start with flows and then do some grouping and categorizing of activities to make sure that I've correctly identified the patterns. Then I hash out the general design direction for whatever it is I'm creating. Other folks skip the flows altogether and focus on the individual interactions, jotting down patterns and trends and figuring out what these might look like and how they might work. If you're working as part of a team, you may want to first compare notes on what you saw, talk about what these mean for your design, and iteratively flow and sketch, correcting and modifying as you go.

The first thing I do, either during or soon after the observation sessions, is flow each individual session into a high-level flowchart.

Michael, Age 3

Time	0:00	0:02
Actions	Picked up toy truck & zoomed it around the floor, making "vroom vroom" noises. Talked about how this is his favorite truck because it is blue and has "big wheels"	Put truck down, picks up "Little People" and acts out a trip to the grocery store (uses a LEGO box as the store)
Objects	Blue truck, crayons, "Little People" figurines	"Little People" - 2 female and 1 child characters; LEGO box
Insights	Runs truck over other toys like crayons and action figures; seems to realize he's running over "people" and thinks it's funny - taking risks in a safe environment, maybe acting out fears?	"Mom" character lets the "child" character buy favorites like strawberries, chips and milk - familiar activity, comfortable, control over purchases
Themes	Independence, control, empowerment, overcoming fear	

Time	0:15	0:22
Actions	Puts away "Telling Time Bingo." Places the cards in the box and scoops the game pieces in on top of them. Puts the clock on top of everything. The box won't close, so he dumps the game pieces out and tries again	Goes to book shelf and takes out 3 books - Sits on the floor and pretends to "read" to me. Tells me the stories in each book, based on the pictures. Tells the stories pretty accurately.
Objects	"Telling Time Bingo"- game pieces, cards, clock and box.	Books - "Goodnight Gorilla," "Hop on Pop" and "Brown Bear, Brown Bear".
Insights	Seems to be slowing down. Spending more time on individual activities. Almost nap time?	Definitely getting tired. Answers all my questions about the books. Thinks it's hilarious that I ask why he thinks the cat is purple - "because his mommy and daddy are purple!"
Themes	Fitting objects into a container; conservation	Storytelling

FIGURE 2.2
A sample observation flowchart.

It usually looks something like Figure 2.2. You'll notice that Michael, age 3, picked up the truck as an action, then moved on to his Little People, played pretend activities that related to his typical day (grocery store, playground, and so on), then switched over to a board game, and finally finished up by "reading" a book.

0:08	0:12
Changes game to "playground" and swings "child" character on a toy swing. Brings in other Little People and pretends they are the other kids on the playground	Leaves Little People on the floor and picks up "Telling Time Bingo". Spins the game's clock around and around. Lays bingo cards out end to end, then side to side. Dumps game pieces on top of the Little People
Little People, male & female characters, fireman, female pilot, swing, truck, minivan	"Telling Time Bingo"- game pieces, cards, clock. Little People
All characters are playing & talking to each other. Trying to tell me about a typical/fun day? Things he likes to do?	He's having a blast. Has no interest in playing the game the "right" way, he's enjoying tactile quality of the cards and the noise the clock makes when it spins. Dumping chips on the figures is hilarious
Fun, friends, connection, interaction	Breaking the rules, making a mess, tactile aspects of objects

0:30

Puts books down, on top of bookshelf. Comes over and gives me a high-five when I tell him he was great and that I learned a lot from him

Books, bookshelf

Gets a little annoyed when his mom tells him it's time to clean up his toys and take a nap. Does a half-hearted job putting books on the bookshelf. She tries to make a game out of it; he is not interested. Nap time.

Control

Next, I jot down the various objects, actions, themes, and insights onto sticky notes or index cards. Then I group them, regroup them, and regroup them again. This technique is called *affinity diagramming*,[5] and helps me understand the kids' most important actions, assumptions, and ideas (see Figure 2.3). It also shows me how I might leverage these when designing my site or app. You'll want to identify a "sweet spot" for your app, say, 3-year-olds, so you can create a baseline for interpretation. Then, using what you know about 3-year-olds (see Chapter 3 on development and cognition), you'll be able to interpret the themes and actions based on this cognitive stage.

FIGURE 2.3
Using affinity
diagramming.

At this point, I create a sort of dictionary of themes and patterns to use when thinking through features and functionality, which helps kick off the ideating stage. I usually do some high-level flows for the main tasks or games to make sure they make sense, and then build out the "cool stuff" from there. Basically, I get everything I need ready to start the "architect" process.

However, if you're working at a company as part of a large, cross-functional team, it's a good idea to schedule ideation workshops as part of the "analyze" step. If your team members observed your absorption sessions, or even if they haven't, chances are they'll help you think about your data in ways that you hadn't considered. You can involve them in affinity diagramming, or just share what you saw and have them help you figure out what it means to the site or app you're creating.

---

5 http://infodesign.com.au/usabilityresources/affinitydiagramming/
   http://www.servicedesigntools.org/tools/23eb

Architect

"Architecting" simply means that you're creating the structure and function of your system. If I'm working with kids over the age of 7, I like to start with some sort of participatory design activity, where I share the basic theme of the app with the kids—as well as some of the trends identified during analysis—and let them come up with their own design prototype. (Catalina Naranjo-Bock gives some great ideas on how to conduct participatory design sessions in her interview at the end of Chapter 9.)

Letting kids "design" their version of your site or app will help you understand the types of interactions they expect to have with your design and how they would like it to function (see Figure 2.4). These sessions have the added benefit of helping you further understand your users' cognitive abilities and expectations around content and flow as well. A cautionary note: Rarely will you take these actual designs from these sessions and implement them. However, you will learn a lot about how kids interpret your initial concepts by doing this type of activity. Just remember that you have to be really clear with kids at the beginning that their ideas may not end up in the final site or app, or else you *will* end up with some disappointed kids.

FIGURE 2.4
With participatory design, kids work together to create designs for a site or an app.

When you are designing for kids, a critical piece is to architect some sort of working prototype on which to build the future app. These early prototypes can take a variety of different forms. For example, the team at Toca Boca takes the notion of architecting literally and builds prototypes from physical objects, such as string on cardboard or pictures cut out of magazines, before they start developing or hashing out all the requirements. It's important to make some sort of interactive experience at this stage, because you get to work through your flows in a hands-on manner. You'll find that it's easier to evolve and flesh out your ideas with a tool that actually works, rather than working with static images on a screen. If I have the opportunity, I sit with a developer and architect the interactions and flows together with that person—two heads are usually better than one.

Once you have an experience that you're relatively sure meets the needs of kids, you're ready to test it out.

Assess

You'll want to do an iterative assessment process when designing for kids, where you create something, evaluate it, and then re-architect it as needed. I guarantee that your first design will fall flat in some areas, simply because, like with adult users, what kids *want* and what they *say* they want (and what they *do* and what they *say* they do) are often quite different. The point of testing at this stage is just to get your prototype in front of kids and watch them use it. You can ask them to complete specific tasks with your prototype, or you can just ask them to play with it and see what they do. You will want to eventually conduct testing with either a functioning digital prototype or an early iteration of a coded site or app as well, to make sure you've properly addressed all the feedback.

It's imperative that you get parental buy-in at this stage. When designing for kids, you're in a bit of a unique situation, in that the user and the customer are not one and the same. Remember the tagline for Kix cereal, "Kid Tested, Mother Approved?" That's a great summary for the goal of this phase. You want kids to test your design to make sure they like it and can use it, but you also want parents to approve of what you designed so that they'll be willing to buy or download it for their kids. And there is a lot of crap (literally) out there that parents do not approve of.

At a workshop I taught recently, a participant (a designer and developer) summed up this phenomenon beautifully. She has three daughters, all of whom love games, she said, "with poop flying, vomit, mucus, and diarrhea everywhere." But, she said, she thinks these games are "disgusting" and refuses to download them from the app store for her kids. She was wondering, as a designer, how to cater to kids' desires without completely alienating parents, who ultimately call the shots in terms of their kids' app consumption. I call this recognizing the "PTR" or the "Parental Threshold for the Revolting." For example, an app that may cross the PTR is "Why Kids Poo" (see Figure 2.5).

FIGURE 2.5
"Why Kids Poo" may cross the PTR—or not, depending on the child and the parents.

My 4-year-old would *love* this app. Unfortunately for her, she will not have the opportunity to play with it, because I find it disgusting. When testing your creation with kids, ask parents to spend a few minutes with it individually as well, and see if you can identify their PTR. This is tricky, because you don't want to ask the basic question,

"Do you find this revolting?" This question will only give you a yes/no answer. Instead, try to develop a script that will reveal the PTR over a few questions. In my experience, the following three questions will surface the PTR pretty quickly:

- What do you like best about this app? What do you think your child will like best? Why?

- What do you like least? How would this influence your decision on whether or not to let your child play with it?

- What, if anything, do you think we should change about it? Why?

You'll know that you've crossed the threshold by the expression on their faces. Some will laugh, and in an effort to appear cool, will tell you they'd allow their kids to play with your app despite the fact that they find the content revolting. Don't believe them. Tone it down. It's hard to say how many parent interviews it will take for you to identify the PTR accurately, as parents have different sensibilities, but you should start seeing patterns among parents of kids the same age after interviewing about seven of them.

It's important to note that the PTR shifts up and down as kids get older. In my experience, parents of 6–9-year-olds have a higher PTR than parents of any other age group, both younger and older. I suspect this is because kids between 6 and 9 are infatuated with all things disgusting, and parents of kids in this age group have become desensitized.

Chapter Checklist

Here's a checklist to test your knowledge about what was discussed in this chapter.

- [ ] Do you understand how kids learn through play and vice versa?
- [ ] Can you explain how designing for kids is different from designing for adults in these areas: challenge, feedback, trust, and change?
- [ ] Do you know how consistency, purpose, surprise, and lagniappes factor in to designing for both kids and adults?
- [ ] Can you describe the "4 *As*" of the Designing for Kids Framework:

  - Absorb?
  - Analyze?
  - Architect?
  - Assess?

- [ ] Do you know what the PTR is and how to tell whether or not you've crossed it?

Now that you've learned how kids play and learn, and walked through a process for designing for and with child audiences, Chapter 3 will dive into the basics about development and cognition.

CHAPTER 3

Development and Cognition

Noah, Age 3

> Knowing reality means constructing systems of transformations that correspond, more or less adequately, to reality.

> —Jean Piaget

It's important for us as designers to have a basic understanding of our users' cognitive abilities. When designing for adults who fall on the "normal" spectrum, we can be pretty confident that they're able to use deductive reasoning, think abstractly, understand common symbols and icons, and anticipate the outcome of their actions, and we can design accordingly. With kids, this is all up for grabs, especially given how rapidly kids develop. Let's take a quick look into the developmental and cognitive skills of kids in different age groups so we can have a common frame of reference when we start talking about design and research.

The World According to Piaget

Jean Piaget was a Swiss psychologist born in the late 19th century (see Figure 3.1). While completing his post-doctoral work in Paris, Piaget took a job at an elementary school where he analyzed the results of intelligence tests. He noticed that younger kids repeatedly struggled with certain types of questions that older kids and adults had no trouble answering. Based on these observations, he decided that younger children weren't necessarily less intelligent than older kids or adults; they just thought about things differently. Piaget focused his research on these cognitive differences and ultimately developed a theory of cognitive "stages" of development, based on age.

"JEAN PIAGET" BY MIRJORAN IS LICENSED UNDER CC BY 2.0

FIGURE 3.1
Jean Piaget, an innovator in education.

According to Piaget, when kids are born, they are in the sensorimotor stage. "Sensorimotor," which means to function with physical senses and movement, refers to the stage when kids "begin to build up direct knowledge of the world around [them], by relating physical actions to perceived results of those actions."[1] They progress through several other stages until they arrive at the formal operational stage, where they can think logically, use abstract reasoning, and see things from perspectives other than their own. Piaget's Theory of Cognitive Development,[2] based on extensive research with children, details the differences in these stages.

NOTE EINSTEIN ON PIAGET

Albert Einstein called Piaget's theory "So simple only a genius could have thought of it."

Piaget maintained that cognitive development progresses from understanding based on physical actions to understanding based on mental operations. He based his theory on four main learning concepts:

- Schemata
- Assimilation
- Accommodation
- Equilibrium

Schemata

Schemata refer to the behaviors that help very young children understand and interpret the world around them. These schemata are actions that a child takes upon an object, to determine its use and purpose. The most basic example of how a schema is formed is the sucking reflex. If an infant picks up an unfamiliar object, he'll immediately put it in his mouth to see how it responds when he sucks on it. This is how he tries to figure out what that object is—if it doesn't fit into his schema for breast or bottle, it's not important to him. As he gains experience, his schemata will progress in development from sucking, to shaking, to dropping, and so forth. And his

---

1 http://www.simplypsychology.org/sensorimotor.html

2 Herbert P. Ginsburg and Sylvia Opper, *Piaget's Theory of Intellectual Development,* 3rd ed. (Englewood Cliffs, NJ: Prentice-Hall, Inc., 1988), viii–264.

understanding and classification of the objects that make up his world will expand as well.

In a virtual environment, we have the opportunity to further develop a child's digital schemata by creating lots of cool elements for him to interact with—items that promote clicking, shaking, tapping, and dragging. These behaviors will help the child learn the gestures and interactions he'll use in the future.

Assimilation

While schemata are how kids classify objects by physically interacting with them, assimilation refers to how children classify objects in their minds, when they see them. So a young child, after seeing and using many bottles over the course of her short lifetime, will be able to look at a bottle (or a picture of a bottle) and identify it as a bottle without needing to suck on it to make that determination.

In his groundbreaking book, *The Design of Everyday Things*, Don Norman uses the term "affordance" to refer to the properties of an object that communicate its intended use.[3] This concept requires a certain level of assimilation—as well as accommodation—in order to hold true. For example, when you see a doorknob, you know you're supposed to turn it to open the door, because you've assimilated the properties of a doorknob from the schemata you developed as a child, when you actually held and turned a doorknob for the first time.

A child will know how to use a bottle (and then a sippy cup, and then a straw) based on the knowledge he assimilated from his schemata. Assimilation is closely related to the concept of accommodation, which is the exciting point when kids figure out deductive logic.

Accommodation

Accommodation is what happens when children modify their existing beliefs about an object based on what they have assimilated.

My favorite example of this is a story I heard from my friend Erin, about the first time her little brother went to the Smithsonian's

---

3 Donald A. Norman, *The Design of Everyday Things: Revised and Expanded Edition* (New York: Basic Books, 2013).

American Museum of Natural History in Washington, DC. They walked into the lobby and saw the huge skeleton of a wooly mammoth. Erin's brother pointed at the skeleton and said, "biiiiig doggie!" He assimilated the visual information in front of him (animal with four legs) into his own interactions with an animal with four legs, which was a dog, and concluded he must be looking at a dog.

When his parents told him that no, in fact, not all animals with four legs are dogs, and that in fact, this was a prehistoric being called a wooly mammoth, he was able to accommodate this information into a new classification in his mind—a giant, prehistoric animal with four legs and two massive tusks, which was much bigger than the elephants at the zoo.

Equilibrium

Equilibrium refers to the balance that people must strike between assimilation and accommodation. As children get older, they have to achieve a balance between when they apply previous knowledge and when they have to account for new knowledge. As they mature, kids get better at accommodating a greater number of variables per object, so they are not classifying things based on only one or two characteristics. When they run out of characteristics to assimilate, they must accommodate objects based on new ones.

In the previous example, when he got more cognitively mature, Erin's brother was able to look at all different kinds of animals with four legs, as well as other characteristics, and determine whether they were something he'd already assimilated, or if they represented something new that he'd have to accommodate for.

Kids struggle with equilibrium as they go through the maturation process. My 5-year-old is convinced that every black car she sees in the parking lot belongs to my husband. She's just starting to look for the Hyundai symbol on the back as she moves toward equilibrium.

> **NOTE** ADULTS AND EQUILIBRIUM
>
> Adults struggle with equilibrium, too! Have you ever been somewhere unfamiliar and, based on a particular building or landmark, think you've been there before? That's your brain trying to decide whether it should assimilate the visual information into an existing category or accommodate it into a new one.

Theory of Cognitive Development

The previous four concepts—schemata, assimilation, accommodation, and equilibrium—make up Piaget's Theory of Cognitive Development. Next, let's take a look at the four stages within this theory:

- Sensorimotor Stage
- Preoperational Stage
- Concrete Operational Stage
- Formal Operational Stage

It's important to note that, while Piaget focused on cognitive development, when designing for kids, you need to look at emotional, physical, and technological development as well. To account for this, in Chapters 4–8, I've broken these cognitive stages into two-year increments to more effectively address the unique needs of children, who evolve quickly across multiple areas. Remember that designing for a 3-year-old is very different than designing for a 6-year-old, even though both these kids fall into the preoperational stage.

The Sensorimotor Stage: From Birth to Age 2

The sensorimotor stage is fascinating because it is the time when kids start figuring out the world and their place in it through their own actions and behaviors. It's important to note here that the American Academy of Pediatrics recommends no screen time (TV, computer, tablet, phone, and so on) until kids reach the age of two, and I agree with this, since these little ones are still discovering the intrinsic properties of the basic physical objects that make up their world. If a plain cardboard box is a super-exciting plaything to babies, then a screen with brightly colored pictures jumping around on it might be a little too much for them to handle. Admittedly, keeping kids away from technology until they're two is a tough proposition. If you're planning to design for the under-two set, here are some key things to remember about this stage.

Separate Selves

When babies are born, they believe that everything in their environment is connected to them. During the sensorimotor stage, they begin to realize that they are not, in fact, so tied to the objects around them, and that they can move and manipulate these objects separately. Babies start experiencing separation anxiety around 8 or 9 months of age when they realize a parent is a separate entity and not simply a ubiquitous extension of themselves.

Object Permanence

The object permanence phase is an important phenomenon of the sensorimotor stage because it's when babies learn that objects and people continue to exist even when they're hidden from view. This is a delightful discovery for babies, and can result in lengthy games of "peek-a-boo" with parents, toys, pets, and, really, anything that can be easily covered with a blanket (see Figure 3.2). When tots learn about object permanence, their separation anxiety tends to lessen a little bit, as they realize their parents still exist even after they leave and will come back for them soon.

FIGURE 3.2
Object permanence means that babies realize objects still exist even when they're hidden from view.

Early Representational Thought

Toward the end of the sensorimotor stage, toddlers are able to start using the schemata they've developed to interpret items in their environment instead of needing to touch and act on everything.

This is important because they are starting to reason and to learn by seeing instead of only by doing. This phenomenon happens between 18 and 24 months of age and propels kids into the next stage, the preoperational stage.

The Preoperational Stage: Ages 2–6

"Preoperational" is a term that Piaget developed to refer to children who don't yet understand "concrete logic" and can only see things from their own point of view. Kids enter the preoperational stage at around age two. This is a very exciting developmental stage, especially for parents, because this is when kids start using language as a communication tool. Even if toddlers aren't speaking at this point, they're probably understanding almost everything they hear, which indicates their ability to associate words with physical objects.

You'll find that this is also a great stage to design for, because it's the stage when kids are able to pretend. A feather duster becomes a magic wand, a towel becomes a cape, and a plate becomes a steering wheel. Toddlers also start acting (playing) out different roles in this stage, like "mommy," "doctor," "pirate," and "fireman" (see Figure 3.3).

"PIRATE PARADE" BY MIKE BAIRD IS LICENSED UNDER CC BY 2.0.

FIGURE 3.3
Kids start playing pretend in the preoperational stage.

As designers, we especially need to observe kids in this stage, because despite the fact that they're developing language skills, they're still not able to clearly articulate their thoughts and behaviors (an issue that continues through adulthood).

Important aspects of this stage include egocentrism and conservation.

Egocentrism

Despite their ability to pretend, children this age have a hard time seeing things from other people's perspectives, and they tend to be very egocentric in their attitude toward life. Piaget conducted an experiment, called "The Three Mountain Test," where he sat kids at a table in front of three 3D mountains and put a doll on the other side of the table. He then asked the children to draw the mountains from the doll's point of view. All the kids in the experiment drew the scene from their own visual perspective, since they couldn't figure out that the view from the other side of the table might be different (see Figure 3.4). In Chapter 4, we'll talk about how to handle this phenomenon when designing for these kids, but suffice it to say, you'll want to present everything from the child's perspective. This is harder than it sounds. Stay tuned.

FIGURE 3.4
Piaget's famous "Three Mountain Test" experiment shows that kids in the preoperational stage can only see things from their own perspective.

Conservation

Since these children aren't yet able to think abstractly, they're only able to understand the visual information in front of them. In Piaget's famous conservation experiment, he poured the same amount of water into two identical containers, in front of a group of kids. Then he took one of the containers and poured it into a taller, thinner container. Even though the kids watched him pour the water into the taller container, they still said the taller container now had more liquid in it, simply because it looked fuller (see Figure 3.5). This perception changes relatively quickly when kids enter the next phase, the concrete operational stage, but it presents challenges when designing for this age group, because you'll have to be very conscious of how you present every piece of visual information.

FIGURE 3.5
In Piaget's conservation experiments, kids were unable to tell that both cylinders held the same amount of water.

The Concrete Operational Stage: Ages 7–11

In the concrete operational stage, children are able to think logically about concrete ideas or events but have difficulty understanding abstract concepts or hypotheses. This means that, while they are starting to understand symbols and representations, it's hard for them to extrapolate meaning using abstract thought. It's a little easier to design for these kids, since you don't have to rely solely on visual examples, but it presents its own set of challenges. For example, you won't be able to use some of the symbols and icons you'd use with an adult audience, so you'll have to make sure your interface communicates its use without these (see Chapter 5).

Important aspects of this phase include inductive logic and reversibility.

Inductive Logic

Piaget found in this stage that children were able to use inductive logic, meaning that they were able to apply reasoning from a specific situation to a larger, more general situation. For example, if you push your friend and your friend gets angry, you learn that people get upset when you push them. However, children this age haven't yet learned to use deductive logic, and understand that, if their friends get upset when they push them, they shouldn't push them.

Reversibility

Despite the lack of deductive reasoning in this age bracket, these kids are starting to be able to reverse their mental categorization. For example, a child may be able to realize that his fish is a betta, and therefore a betta is a fish, and a fish is a type of animal.

The Formal Operations Stage: Ages 12–Adult

We all know how to design for people in the formal operations stage. It's the people you design for every day—your adult users whom you know so well (or try to, at least). The important hallmarks of this stage are the development of logical thought, deductive reasoning, and complex problem solving.

You'll want to consider the following areas when designing for this phase: logic, abstract thought, and problem solving.

Logic

According to Piaget, logic refers to the ability to use general concepts to solve a specific problem. Remember those algebra classes in middle school? The reason you had to take them, even though you were way more interested in art and drama, was to hone your deductive reasoning skills. So while you may never have to solve for x as an adult, you use the logic you developed almost every day.

Abstract Thought

Surviving as an adult requires the ability to hypothesize about the potential outcomes of one's actions and decisions. Children develop this cognitive skill at around age 12. This means that, instead of relying on past experiences as the basis of their decisions, kids are able to think hypothetically about their options. These skills are essential for future planning.

Problem Solving

Before they reach the formal operations stage, children use trial-and-error to solve problems. In the formal operations stage, kids are able to draw on logic and deduction to develop solutions to complex problems. When you design for adults, you tend to (correctly) assume that they have this ability, unless you design for special populations.

Chapter Checklist

Here's a checklist to test your knowledge about what was discussed in this chapter.

☐ Do you understand how Jean Piaget's Theory of Cognitive Development helps illustrate the cognitive abilities of kids of different ages?

☐ Can you explain the following four concepts that support this theory?

- Schemata: Behaviors that identify objects and their purposes.

- Assimilation: Identification of objects based on their physical attributes.

- Accommodation: Classification of objects based on multiple attributes.

- Equilibrium: The balance between assimilation and accommodation.

☐ Can you describe the following Stages of Cognitive Development?

- Sensorimotor Stage: From birth–2, kids start to figure out the objects that make up their world.

- Preoperational Stage: From 2–6, children are egocentric and only understand concepts and objects as they relate to them.

- Concrete Operations Stage: From 7–11, kids start to use inductive logic to solve problems.

- Formal Operations Stage: 12 and up, children can use abstract thought and deductive reasoning to gain knowledge.

In this book, we're going to draw on the principles described here to explain how to design for children of different ages. In the next chapter, we'll take a look at kids in the early preoperational stage, from 2–4.

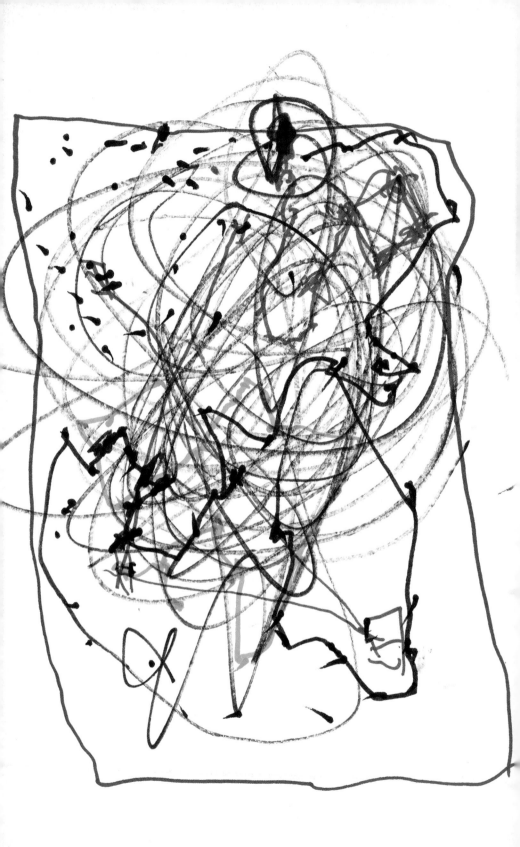

CHAPTER 4

Kids 2–4: Little People, Big Expectations

Emerson or Easton, twins, Age 4

We must teach our children to dream with their eyes open.

—Harry Edwards

Kids between ages 2 and 4 are fascinating. They're transforming from babies into real little people. They're developing opinions, preferences, and personalities of their own. They're starting to express their feelings through words. And they're wonderful to design for, because they haven't yet formed assumptions about how the world should work.

In this chapter, we'll talk about how to design for these kids. We'll look at who they are, what they like, and how to create experiences that appeal to their physical, emotional, and cognitive skills.

Who Are They?

Let's take a look at some key characteristics in Table 4.1 that shape the behavior and attitudes of 2–4-year-olds and how these might impact your design decisions.

When creating experiences for 2–4-year-olds, you'll need to remember that these kids are just figuring out how to use technology. They haven't developed expectations about how things should work yet. You'll have lots of opportunities to be creative with this group, but you may need to reconsider some basic visual and interaction design principles in order to design an experience that meets their needs.

Let's go through each of the items in Table 4.1 to understand the implications that these elements have when designing for 2–4-year-olds.

Create a Clear Visual Ranking

Children in this age group can't easily tell what the "important" parts of an interface are. They tend to click on just about everything to see what happens; it's all part of the game for them. So you'll want to create a strong visual separation between the elements that users can interact with and those they can't.

Let's look at two examples from kids' TV show websites. The first example, from the *Caillou* website, shows how a clear hierarchy makes it easy for kids to tell what they're supposed to click on. The second example, *Angelina Ballerina*, shows what happens without this visual ranking and how this can be confusing for young children.

TABLE 4.1 CONSIDERATIONS FOR 2–4-YEAR-OLDS

2-4-year-olds...	This means that...	You'll want to...
Focus on details instead of the "big picture."	They can't distinguish main elements of an interface from the details.	Create a very clear visual distinction between interactive items and design extras.
Can rank items by only one characteristic at a time (i.e., color, shape, and so on).	They get overwhelmed when there are too many variables competing for their attention.	Pick a smallish set of easily identifiable elements (like colors) and use them consistently throughout your design.
Can only associate a single function with an item or object.	If an item expands or makes a sound on rollover, they'll believe that's the sole purpose of that item and won't know to click on it.	Limit the behavior of your navigation elements to navigation (for example, don't have them pop up or make noise).
Can only see items on a screen in two dimensions, not three.	Everything on a screen looks like it's in a single, flat plane to them.	Make your foreground items much clearer and more detailed than stuff in the background.
Are just learning to think abstractly.	They are unable to understand icons and symbols that are second nature to adults.	Use icons that are highly representative of the task you're trying to communicate.
Use sound to identify items in their environment.	They get confused when different sounds have different meanings (for example, a police siren and an ambulance siren).	Make sure that every sound you use has a specific meaning and function.
Are starting to develop their own identity.	They develop a sense of self at around age 2, complete with gender identity, which forms very early.	Create a design that allows for gender identification without forcing kids down a specific gender path.

On the *Caillou* site, kids can launch mini-games from items in the environment. Almost all the elements on the site react in some way, but only the ones with the white borders have games associated with them (see Figure 4.1). This visual distinction is easy to recognize, even without the accompanying voice prompts.

In Figure 4.1, the dollhouse and train, which have white borders, launch games when clicked. The items without the borders (for example, the rug, sun, and bookshelf) animate when users mouse over them, but they don't open any additional functionality. This distinction makes it easy for kids to learn how to access the games and to remember what to do on return visits.

FIGURE 4.1
It's easy to see that items with white borders on the *Caillou* site will launch games.

It's important to note that kids under age 6 tend to associate only *one* behavior or action with an object, which means that to an average 4-year-old, if something on the screen moves when he touches it, that's all it's supposed to do. So you'll want to make sure that your navigational items look clickable, but don't do anything too interesting to detract from their purpose. We'll explore this in more detail later in this chapter.

On the *Angelina Ballerina* site, children can launch various activities by clicking the windows in the schoolhouse; however, it's really hard to figure this out. Only by mousing over the windows and waiting for an overlay to pop up can users tell if there is an activity there or not (see Figures 4.2 and 4.3). This visual hierarchy is confusing to kids, because everything on the screen looks the same and seems to be of the same level of importance.

FIGURE 4.2

On the *Angelina Ballerina* site, kids have to roll over the windows to find out how to play the games.

FIGURE 4.3

The overlay with words on *Angelina Ballerina* is the only way that users know they can play a game. Unfortunately, most of these users don't read yet.

If the clickable windows in the above screens were highlighted or differentiated in some way, it would be easier for kids to know what to do. For example, if the mice in the windows were dancing, or were dressed in brighter colors, or were a bit larger, children would know that something would happen if they clicked on them. Currently, their size and colors blend in with the pale background, which makes them hard for a young child to see.

Kids haven't cultivated the visual filtering skills adults have. They're unable to understand hierarchy unless it's clearly communicated through visual indicators. If your interactive elements aren't prominent enough, kids will have to learn what to click on through trial and error, and you'll run the risk of alienating and possibly losing your audience.

Use a Few Bright Colors

There is a popular misconception among designers that kids like lots of colors. It's true that younger children love things that are bright and bold, but actually they prefer a limited color palette and can get overwhelmed if there are too many colors competing for their attention. Because kids between ages 2 and 4 hone in on details instead of the big picture, a design with lots of different colors and shades, as well as textures, makes it harder for them to figure out what to click on.

Let's look at an iPhone app called *Smack That Gugl* (see Figure 4.4) to see how the developers have creatively limited their color palette to increase usability for kids.

FIGURE 4.4
Smack That Gugl does a great job using a limited palette with bright colors.

The premise of *Smack That Gugl* is very simple: smack the creatures before they explode. The designers of this app used just five colors for their interface. By positioning bright colorful elements on a plain white background, they made it easy for kids to know what to click and touch. If they had used any additional colors, even within the same color family, it would have increased the visual complexity for kids and made it difficult for them to use. Older children look for more visual excitement when it comes to color and texture, but younger ones prefer simplicity.

Color serves as the primary "preattentive variable" for 2–4-year-olds, meaning that they mentally categorize items based on color instead of size, shape, or location. This is true for adults, too, but adults have the ability to continue to categorize cognitively based on other factors as well.

In a similar game called *Smack Match Gugl* (see Figure 4.5), kids can play against the device, sliding Gugls to the opposite side of the "field" before they explode. The designers rely on color alone—as opposed to shape, size, or orientation—to differentiate between the two "teams" of Gugls. This colorizing puts much less cognitive burden on little users, as they can easily identify which Gugls are on their team and which are not. It also ensures a greater level of success for them as they play the game.

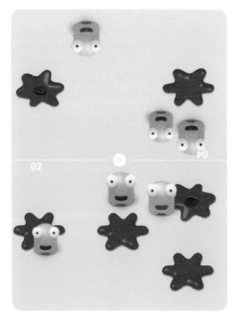

FIGURE 4.5
Smack Match Gugl
uses color to help
its young users
categorize.

Designing Touch Interfaces for Younger Kids

Children ages 2–4 are the perfect audience for touch-based interfaces, simply because they haven't been tainted by years of poorly designed screen interfaces like adults have. However, these kids also haven't been exposed to a tremendous number of real-world gestures yet either, so designing touch interfaces for these young users can be complicated. For example, kids think of "pinching" as either (1) picking up a small object or (2) something you do to your friend when you're mad at her, not as a way to shrink an on-screen element. In addition, these little ones are still a bit clumsy, so some of the finer gestures are difficult for them to master.

When designing touch interfaces for younger ones, you'll want to do the following:

- Focus on large, broad gestures instead of small, fine ones. Try using swiping and grabbing instead of pinching and flicking.

- Make on-screen elements big enough for kids to manipulate. This can be hard on smaller screens. You'll want to do some testing to make sure that items are large enough for little hands

- When possible, make use of full hand gestures instead of relying on the thumb and index finger alone. Kids under age 5 tend to use their whole hand to scroll instead of just a single finger.

- Place navigation controls at the bottom of the screen, in the left and right corners to indicate the forward and backward motion. Make these large and easy for clumsy thumbs to tap. Kids under age 5 won't recognize left- and right-facing arrows as progression, but they will realize that right means forward and left means back (in Western cultures, at least).

There are plenty of offline gestures kids are comfortable with, like turning pages in a book or rubbing a crayon on a piece of paper. Just make sure the gestural metaphors you choose map to ones your young users already know.

As adorable as the Gugl game is, it makes a lot (*A LOT*) of noise. It also occasionally pops up messages asking the user to sign in to the GameCenter. For parents who "pass it back"—for example, hand tablets and smartphones over to kids as a form of distraction for a long car trip or in a restaurant—it's really annoying to have to constantly reach back and close a dialog box or correct an error. These messages can have financial and privacy implications as well, particularly when they ask for access to *Facebook* accounts, photos, location data, or permission for the user to make in-app store purchases. When designing apps for kids, make sure there are "set it and forget it" parental controls for things like volume, upsells, and messaging so that parents can set their preferences once and hand the device over without worry.

Assign a Single Behavior to On-Screen Elements

I did some in-home interviews with 2- and 3-year-olds last year and asked them to show me their favorite toys. Most of these favorites were toys with electronic components, like toy laptops, cell phones, or dolls that spoke or sang. When I asked the kids to show me how the toy worked, most of them showed me a single feature of the toy, like a noise it made when they pushed a particular button, or an action it performed when they shook or squeezed it.

The follow-up conversations with parents were very interesting:

"We spent all this money on a toy tablet for Gabriella, but she only does one or two things with it," said Gabby's mom. "She likes to push the picture of the fish and hear it say 'fish.' In fact, she calls it her 'fishie machine.'"

"My parents got Leo this little computer," said Leo's mother. "It's supposed to teach him letters and colors and words. There's one button that makes a loud honking noise when you push it. That's the only thing this child will do with this computer. He hasn't learned anything from it, I don't think. A waste of money, if you ask me."

This tendency, to associate a single behavior with an object or item, manifests itself in digital environments as well. If an element on-screen makes a noise or jumps around when the child rolls over it, the child is going to think that's the sole purpose of the element. This becomes especially problematic when designing navigation.

Many designers think that in order to get a child to click on something, that thing needs to attract her attention. As a result, we see navigation buttons highlight, move, and chime on rollover. Unfortunately, that will make young children less likely to click them, as they'll believe their only function is to highlight, move, or chime. Let's look at an example.

Daniel Tiger's Neighborhood is a wonderful TV show with a great companion website that has activities and games for the under-four crowd. Its designers fell into the familiar trap, however, of creating navigation that reacts when a child mouses over it (or, on a mobile device, taps it a single time.) Take a look at the "Printables" button in Figure 4.6. The top navigation bar shows the default state of the button, and the bottom bar shows the expanded and angled button that appears when the user places her mouse on it, on the desktop site.

FIGURE 4.6
Keep navigation static so kids won't get confused about its purpose.

Interestingly, when a child uses the *Daniel Tiger's Neighborhood* site on a tablet, the navigation changes appear when the child taps an icon, requiring two taps to actually navigate to that section of the site. This further reinforces the idea that the only purpose these images serve is to get bigger and shift position, as that's all they do when tapped.

I actually witnessed this phenomenon first-hand during a baseline usability test of a kids' website (and have seen it many times since.)

When designing the site, we thought it would be cute to have the characters in the navigation pop up and make a sound when users rolled over them. During the test, kids got so excited when they saw the characters jumping around that they forgot to actually click on the items to see more content.

Bottom line: If you feel compelled to add audio and animation to your navigation because you think kids might not understand it, you may need to revisit the design of your buttons.

Maintain a Strong Separation Between Foreground and Background

Children are able to see things in 3D starting at around 5 months of age, when both their eyes start working at the same time;[1] however, they can't really visualize a 3D experience on a flat screen until they're almost 5 years old.[2] As a result, it's hard to figure out how to position elements so as to give them context. You'll want to make a realistic-looking interface, so these very literal-minded users understand what's going on, but it's better to focus on using color and detail for foreground (important) elements and rely on simple shapes and muted colors for background (secondary) elements, instead of designing a fully realized environment.

Figure 4.7 highlights *Little Pim Spanish* for iPad, where you'll see that the Panda characters are brighter and more detailed than the background. There is enough visual information in the background to communicate context and representation (for example, you can tell you're outside on the grass), but it has limited texture and detail to help kids understand that those things are less important.

Let's contrast that with *Handy Manny's Workshop* (see Figure 4.8). This interface will look very flat to a young child. The main characters in the toolbox blend into the background simply because they are at the same level of fidelity as the rest of the screen, which makes it hard for kids to understand what's in the front and what's in the back. Instead, it will all look like a lot of clutter, and young users will have a hard time figuring out what to tap.

---

1 http://www.aoa.org/patients-and-public/good-vision-throughout-life/childrens-vision/infant-vision-birth-to-24-months-of-age

2 http://www.visionandhealth.org/documents/Child_Vision_Report.pdf

FIGURE 4.7

Little Pim Spanish uses less color and detail in the background to help kids focus on the important parts of the interface.

FIGURE 4.8

Handy Manny's Workshop has a very detailed background, which will make it difficult for kids to identify what it is they need to do.

Make Literal Use of Pictures and Icons

Kids ages 2–4 are just beginning to understand abstract thought. As a result, icons and images common to adults can confuse them. By the age of 3, most of them understand that clicking on an "X" closes a window, and that left- and right-pointing arrows move forward and backward, but this behavior is learned, not understood.

Of course, kids in this age group can't read, so pictures and icons are even more important. As a general rule of thumb, if you need more than a word or two to describe how something is supposed to work, the interaction is too complicated. You know you're on the right track if you can identify a representative symbol to communicate your task.

TIP KEEP IT SIMPLE

You'll know your design is too complicated for 2–4-year-olds if it needs text or audio instructions. Any design—or part of a design—requiring more than a couple of words to describe what kids are supposed to do needs to be re-thought.

The *Nick Jr.* website uses iconography that's probably confusing to a lot of young children. Take this control panel from the *Backyardigans* section, for example (see Figure 4.9.) The game's icon, a video game controller, isn't a great choice here, because it represents a specific interaction model unrelated to the website. Kids of this age group

FIGURE 4.9
Nick Jr.'s control panel has confusing iconography.

may not have even seen a video game controller like this before, as game systems like Nintendo and XBOX target older kids. A better choice would have been an image of a child playing a computer or tablet game, to give the users some information about the types of things they'll see in that section.

The video icon is confusing, too. Young children don't yet understand that a green, left-facing arrow means "play." Also, as we discussed in Chapter 2, "Playing and Learning," since these kids only see things from their own perspective, they'll look for something that implies *watching* a video, not *playing* a video. The difference is subtle, but important. A TV or video monitor would be a better option here.

Some other options for common icons include the following examples in Table 4.2

TABLE 4.2 APPROPRIATE ICONS FOR 2-4-YEAR-OLDS

Action	Symbol	Description
Print		A piece of paper with a picture on it
Favorite/Save		A heart or a star
Start		A finger pointing
Finish/End		A stop sign
Share		Two people sharing something between them
Volume		An ear, with "sound waves" coming out from it. No sound waves = no sound; 3 sound waves = loudest sound

Designing Icons for Children

For Chapter 10 of this book, I designed a video app to demonstrate how interfaces need to change for kids of different ages. As part of this exercise, I wanted to use a set of icons to represent different subject areas. This ended up being more difficult than I expected, because I needed concrete imagery to represent abstract topics like "communication." I worked with an illustrator, Shelby Bertsch, on these icons, and we went back and forth several times, as it took awhile to find pictures that did an adequate job of representing the concepts I wanted to include. Looking at the pictures below, you can see how the pictures represent the following topics:

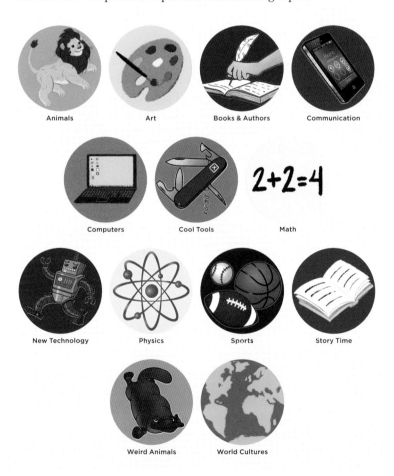

Animals Art Books & Authors Communication

Computers Cool Tools Math

New Technology Physics Sports Story Time

Weird Animals World Cultures

These icons shown in the sidebar may not seem intuitive to you, but that's because you're able to think abstractly, and you're already used to common symbols used in interface design. To a child under 4, these make a lot of sense.

You'll notice that some of these icons—like the heart and the stop sign—are actually symbols, as opposed to real representations of the actions. However, kids learn these symbols at an early age and have already assimilated them into their cognitive toolbox. When choosing your icons, you'll want to make sure that you take this into consideration. And, of course, you'll want to evaluate and test your icon choices with actual kids during the "assess" stage of the process.

Use Clear Audio Cues

Some designers believe that, when designing for young children, everything has to make noise. While it's true that these younger users like auditory feedback, there has to be a method to the madness. Sound needs to communicate, inform, and instruct, as opposed to simply entertain. It's better to identify specific conventions for sound types and stick to those rather than to have noises coming from all over the place. This principle is true because kids of this age are only able to associate a single response or action to an element.

You'll need to be strategic when thinking about how to use audio in your interface. First, identify the types of sounds you want to include, and then figure out a single use for each type. Table 4.3 shows a sample inventory chart that may help you plan how to identify your sounds.

If you're planning on having lots of sounds, you may want to create a more detailed inventory with columns for characters, elements, specific actions, and so on. Establishing audio conventions relatively early in the design process will help ensure that you use sounds consistently and appropriately, which will in turn help your young users figure out how to use your design. Let's look at an example.

Sago Mini Sound Box is a phenomenal app designed for toddlers and preschoolers. What makes this app great is that it lets kids interact with the entire device, not just images on the screen. This specific interaction helps improve the child's gross and fine motor skills and teaches some basic physics concepts as well. The premise is simple:

TABLE 4.3 SAMPLE INVENTORY OF SOUNDS

Sound Type	Description	Use
Voice-over	Brief sound bites from characters, no more than five-word sentences	Instruction/explanation/invitation (for example, "Touch the ball to play!")
Music	Short (1–2 seconds), upbeat, continuous tunes	Beginning/completing a task (for example, winning a game, starting a new activity, leaving a virtual space)
Beep	Quick single beep sound	"Time's Up" or "Try Again"
Doorbell	Loud "Ding-Dong"	When a new character or element enters the screen
Click	Very brief, smooth single click sound	User action (for example, moving a game piece, pressing a key, or selecting a navigation item)

kids first select a sound category and then create different sounds by tapping to add multi-colored circles, which, when dragged, crack open to reveal various friendly household animals. Kids can make all sorts of collective noises by shaking, swishing, and rotating their device so that the circles whirl around and ricochet off the sides of the screen. (Incidentally, this app captivates middle-aged adults as well.)

Mini Sound Box does a great job with its audio cues, which is especially difficult, given that it's a sound-creation toy. The designers created a very clear distinction between system sounds and sounds produced by kids as part of the game (see Figure 4.10.) In fact, they limited their system sounds to only the essential pieces of functionality (adding a circle, opening a circle, tapping an animal) and let the kids create the rest of the sounds within the app experience itself. There are no extraneous sounds for selecting a category or navigating back to the landing screen, just little sound files communicating progress to keep kids engaged.

Mini Sound Box features a home screen with no verbal or written instructions, which is an extremely difficult feat. An upbeat song plays when kids open the app, to let them know it's working and ready for them to play. Big pictures with familiar images enable kids to engage with the app immediately, but tapping these images doesn't produce additional noise. It just takes kids to the next screen, which shows an adorable cartoon animal ushering in one of the sound circles (see Figure 4.11).

FIGURE 4.10

Mini Sound Box uses specific sounds to communicate progress and functionality.

FIGURE 4.11

A short animation introduces the concept of sound circles to kids using the app.

Kids can tap anywhere on the screen to add additional sound circles. Depending on the category initially selected, the sounds can be percussion instruments, piano chords, barks, tweets, meows, or cars and trucks. Any movement of the device itself zooms the circles around the screen, releasing a cacophony of wonderfully discordant sounds (see Figure 4.12.)

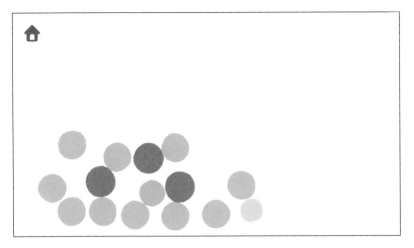

FIGURE 4.12

Mini Sound Box helps children work on their fine motor skills by letting them interact with the entire device.

What makes this an all-around great app for preschoolers, in addition to its clear audio cues, is that it promotes exploration and discovery, has a flow but allows for non-linear play, and provides rewarding visual and auditory feedback with every interaction.

Another wonderful aspect of this app is that it works for kids around the globe, as the sounds used don't require knowledge of any specific language or culture.

Support, Don't Enforce, Gender Differences

Children begin to identify gender at around age 2. A child who likes to play with neutral items, like blocks and balls, may start choosing baby dolls and dress-up clothes or superheroes and cars at this age. Neuroscientist Lise Eliot, in her book *Pink Brain, Blue Brain*,[3] explains that these differences in gender identification come from small competency differences in infant brains that are then reinforced by adults. For example, boys' brains develop certain types of spatial reasoning skills earlier than girls' brains, while baby girls make eye contact earlier and

3 Lise Elliot. *Pink Brain, Blue Brain: How Small Differences Grow Into Troublesome Gaps—And What We Can Do About It* (New York, NY: Houghton Mifflin Harcourt Publishing Company, 2010).

develop the ability to empathize and communicate earlier. The result? "Boys are better at math," and "girls are more nurturing."

At around age 2, children will start developing their own rules for gender behavior (for example, boys like Batman and girls like Cinderella.)

So what does this mean in terms of design? If you're creating a site meant to appeal to both genders, you'll want to make sure that you have an equal balance of activities requiring spatial skills and promoting exploration. Keep the characters gender-neutral, like the Gugls, or create an even balance of male and female characters. It's a good idea, if you're able, to make your characters non-human, like Disney does with it's *Jungle Junction* (see Figure 4.13.)

While these animals have genders, they don't base their actions on their genders. This design allows children to identify with the characters without siloing themselves into gender-specific behavior patterns.

FIGURE 4.13
Disney's *Jungle Junction* features animals instead of humans.

Here are some interesting insights from kids, which were gathered during a series of user research sessions that I did from 2009 to 2010.

Me: "Who's that on your dress?"

Sydney, age 3: "Umm" (pause) "Ryan has a Superman shirt, and I have a Snow White dress because I am a girl and a princess is a girl."

Me: "And what's Superman?"

Sydney: "Superman is a boy." (pause) "He is funny. I like Snow White."

Me: "What do you see on the computer?"

Connor, age 4: "Umm... a car. It's blue."

Me: "What do you think would happen if you clicked on the car?"

Connor: "It would drive fast! I like to go fast. All my guys like to go fast."

Me: "Who are your guys?"

Connor: "My friends, Ryan and Tyler." (pause) "Lily is my friend, too. She likes cars that are pink."

Me: "What else does Lily like?"

Connor: "She is a girl. She likes pink and flowers and dolls."

When I spoke with parents after the sessions, most stated that they didn't start buying gender-specific toys until their child started asking for them, at around age 2.

Ava's mother: "I never really thought about it, but I guess we only recently started giving Ava (age 2) princess stuff. When she was a baby, she had a couple of dolls, but was always more interested in her stuffed bear. She saw a Cinderella doll at a birthday party a few weeks ago and has been asking for one ever since. So we're giving her one for Christmas. She got Ariel pajamas and a Snow White dress-up dress for her second birthday."

Connor's mother: "We tried very hard to keep all gender-specific toys out of our home. We didn't want Connor to feel as though he had to play with cars and fire trucks just because he was a boy. But now he loves Batman and Spiderman. It's almost like a force beyond our control."

Chapter Checklist

Before we move on to designing for 4–6-year-olds, here's a checklist to help you if you're developing sites or apps for younger kids:

Does your design cover the following areas?

☐ Clearly highlight items the child can interact with?

☐ Use only a few colors?

☐ Feature static navigation that doesn't react unless tapped?

☐ Have a clear distinction between foreground and background items?

☐ Use icons that are highly representational?

☐ Use sounds judiciously to communicate function and meaning?

☐ Relate to kids, regardless of gender?

In the next chapter, we'll see some shifts in cognition and behavior as we look at slightly older kids and learn how to design for them.

Favorite App: *LEGO Minifigures Game*

Noah, an adorable bundle of boy, worships everything his 6-year-old brother does. When his brother started playing with LEGO bricks, Noah wanted to play too, but the little pieces were too small for him to actually build anything of substance. He enjoyed playing with DUPLO blocks (essentially, larger LEGO bricks), but he didn't have the level of concentration to play with them for more than a few minutes at a time.

Noah's father downloaded some LEGO-themed apps, and Noah immediately gravitated to the *Minifigures* game, which allows kids to match up the different parts of a minifig and collect entire series. Noah loves the big buttons, the sounds, and, most of all, making crazy mixed-up minifigs (see Figure 4.14).

FIGURE 4.14
LEGO *Minifigures* game lets kids mix-and-match their own characters.

sidebar continues on next page

Noah had a hard time answering my questions while he was playing, but when he showed me his father's iPhone, he kept saying
"Series! Series!" I didn't quite understand what he meant, but then
he quickly navigated to the app, opened it, and showed me how
he used it to build minifigs. When Noah "correctly" completed a
minifig (see Figure 4.15), he showed me the character screen and
then the series page, which had a collection of all the minifigs he'd
completed to date.

"This is my series," he said proudly. "These are my guys!"

FIGURE 4.15
Noah loves collecting
minifigs and adding
them to the app.

The main themes that surfaced during my time with Noah
included discovery, creation, irreverence, and experimentation,
with accomplishment a very distant second. He just loved playing
on the iPhone and creating funny characters. He understood that
the ultimate goal of the game was to add items to his "series," but
like most 2–4-year-olds, his main focus was on the play itself.

Emil Ovemar

Producer and Co-Founder, Toca Boca

Emil Ovemar is the producer and cofounder of Toca Boca, a play studio that makes digital toys for kids. Toca Boca has released 17 titles since its inception in 2010, including the award-winning Toca Tea Party, Toca Kitchen, *and* Toca Robot Lab. *Its newest game,* Toca Tailor, *won a 2013 iKids Award for "Best Game App—6 and Up." Emil lives in Stockholm with his wife, Frida, and kids Abbe and Annie.*

DLG: I love the concept of "digital toys." How did this idea (and Toca Boca) come about? How did you decide to make this your focus?

EO: My colleague Bjorn Jeffery and I worked together at a company called Bonnier Group in 2009. He and I were charged with coming up with prototypes and new ideas for existing, traditional media such as magazines and books, but we wanted to do something new. We looked at all the different options and asked ourselves, "What are people already willing to pay for?" When the topic of creating something for kids came up, I was excited, since I had two kids—ages 5 and 3 at the time—and was starting to see how technology could enter their lives. Parents are willing to pay for educational toys and experiences to help their kids, and I saw this as an opportunity to work on something I was interested in that could benefit kids.

I've always been interested in the ideas of play and fun, and to design something that incorporated these interests in a visually entertaining way was exciting to me. I did some research on what we could do to engage kids, and what I found was not very interesting. Most of the apps available for kids were either simple games or straight instructional experiences. In observing my kids with my iPhone, I saw that they used the device itself as a toy, and they didn't seek out particular games or apps. They liked the sounds it played when they touched different buttons and the animations it played when they switched screens. I thought, why can't we create something that kids can just play with? Why can't we make a toy from the technology itself?

This led to some explorations around creating a new type of toy, and as a result, a new way to play, using advances in touch-screen technology. Toca Boca was born from these explorations (see Figure 4.16).

DLG: Where do your ideas for games come from? How do you decide which ones to build?

EO: We start with a broad concept and theme and then identify opportunities for play within that theme. For example, with *Toca Hair Salon*, although hair salons are associated with fashion and beauty, we wanted to focus on the fun things that could happen when you play and interact with hair (see Figure 4.17).

FIGURE 4.16
Toca Band lets kids make music in unexpected ways.

FIGURE 4.17
Toca Hair Salon lets kids do interesting things with hair.

So we created a bunch of characters, each with a different type of hair, and then focused on all the different things you could do, like cutting, dyeing, washing, and shaving. We concentrated on making these micro-interactions as fun and interesting as possible. So the theme serves as the vehicle for the play, but then the smaller aspects of the theme become the actual game.

DLG: How do you involve kids into your design and development process? What kinds of participatory design activities do you conduct? How much do kids influence what you build and why?

EO: We involve kids throughout the design process. In the beginning, after we identify our concept and theme, we create paper prototypes for small, small aspects of the experience. We use plain paper, or sometimes we use strings on cardboard, and then we put it in front of kids and watch what they do. If they don't respond, we go back and ask ourselves what we need to change, about either the theme or the interactions.

Sometimes, we'll put real physical toys in front of kids and then watch them and ask questions. When we were building *Toca Train*, we gave kids toy trains and just watched how the kids interacted with them and the different things they were trying to do. We kept asking ourselves, what is it that the toymakers have missed that we can do in a digital space? How can we hack the notion of play so kids can do more interesting things?

A great example of this happened when we were working on *Toca Tea Party*. I cut out a bunch of pictures—of teacups, plates, utensils—and then laid them out on the floor in front of my kids. I thought about things that might happen at a real tea party that might be interesting and unexpected. When I was pouring the juice, I pretended that some had spilled, and the kids loved it. That made me think about how to incorporate these fun little "conflicts" into the overall experience. Kids are great at uncovering these because of their ability to hone in on details.

DLG: What are the most important differences between designing for adults and designing for kids?

EO: When we think about designing for adults, or designing games for adult audiences, we usually think of them having some purpose. For example, there are games that adults play to help them with behavior change, or things that they do to earn badges in a gamification environment. But there are very few things adults do digitally for pure enjoyment. That's a major difference. Kids learn, communicate, and grow through play itself, whereas adults usually need a larger purpose for doing so.

Another thing that's different is that feedback is really important when designing for kids. All kinds of feedback. Adults prefer feedback when they do something wrong, or to confirm when they do something right. Kids like to get feedback from a system whenever they do anything at all. They like it when something fun and unexpected happens. Adults don't tend to like the unexpected. Also, the idea of friction is different from kids to adults. Adults do not like friction; they like the tasks to be as straightforward as possible. With kids, they like a little friction, a little challenge. For kids, something like pouring juice or stacking boxes in a digital environment should have an element of adventure to it. Adults just want to get it done. ∎

CHIMÄSEBASTIAN

Kids 4–6: The "Muddy Middle"

Sebastian, Age 4

A little nonsense now and then is relished by the wisest men.

—Roald Dahl

I call kids between ages 4 and 6 the "muddy middle," because they're stuck right in between the cute, cuddly preschool children and the savvy, sophisticated elementary-schoolers. They're too old for games designed for toddlers, but they can't quite read yet, so they struggle with sites and apps geared toward older kids. Unfortunately, you rarely see a digital product designed specifically for this age group, because they're hard to pin down, but these little guys are full of ideas, knowledge, creativity, and charisma.

Like the 2–4s, these children are still in the preoperational stage, but they present their own set of design challenges based on where they are cognitively, physically, and emotionally.

Who Are They?

Table 5.1 shows some key characteristics that shape the behavior and attitudes of 4–6-year-olds and how these might impact your design decisions.

You'll find that 4–6-year-olds have learned "the rules" for how to behave, how to communicate, and how to play. Now they're looking for ways to bend and break these rules. They understand limitations—angry parents, broken toys, and sad friends have taught them well—but they still take every opportunity to test these limitations. Digital environments provide a perfect place for these active kids to challenge the status quo and learn more about the world around them.

Make It Social

When you think of social design for adults, you may think of experiences that let users communicate and interact with others. The same is true of social design for kids, but in this case, "others" doesn't have to mean other kids or even other humans. It means that kids need to feel like part of the experience, and they need to be able to observe and understand the interactions of characters in the experience, as players and contributors. Kids at this age understand that individual differences, feelings, and ideas are important and exciting. Showcasing these differences within the experience and directly

TABLE 5.1 CONSIDERATIONS FOR 4-6-YEAR-OLDS

4-6-year- olds...	This means that...	You'll want to...
Are empathetic.	They're beginning to see things from other perspectives.	Make interactions feel more "social," even if the kids aren't actually communicating with others.
Have an intense curiosity about the world.	They're very interested in learning new ideas, activities, and skills, but may become frustrated when that learning takes longer than they would like.	Set attainable goals for the tasks and activities you create. Provide context-based help and support so kids have an easier time processing information.
Are easily sidetracked.	They sometimes have trouble following through on a task or activity.	Keep activities simple, short, and rewarding. Provide feedback and encouragement after milestones.
Have wild imaginations.	They prefer to create on their own rather than following strict instructions or step-by-step directions.	Make "rules" for play/ engagement as basic as possible and allow for a lot of invention, self-expression, and storytelling.
Are developing increased memory function.	Can recall complex sequences of events just by watching someone perform them.	Include multi-step activities and games, with more than one main goal (for example, touch the red stars and green apples to get points of different values).

communicating with users allows this social aspect to come through and provide additional depth and context to interactions.

Sometimes, making something feel social is as easy as presenting it in the first person. When characters, elements, and instructions speak directly to kids, it makes it easier for them to empathize and immerse themselves in the experience.

Let's take a look at an example from *Seussville*. The designers of this highly engaging site keep the uniqueness of Dr. Seuss's characters vibrantly alive in their lovely character chooser. Every character (and I do mean *every*) from every Dr. Seuss book glides by on whimsical conveyor belts, letting the user pick one to play with (see Figure 5.1).

This character chooser provides a strong social experience for kids, because it allows them to "meet" and build relationships with the individual characters. Kids can control the viewer, from a first-person perspective, to see the visual differences among the characters, as well as personality details that make the characters unique, much like how they'd go about meeting people in real life (without the conveyor belt, of course).

When users choose a character, they are shown a quote, a book list, and details about the character on the pull-down screen to the right. On the left side of the screen, a list of games and activities featuring the character magically appears.

FIGURE 5.1
Seussville presents a first-person perspective to kids.

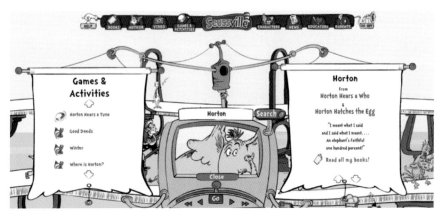

FIGURE 5.2
Seussville feels social, even though kids don't interact with other humans.

This social experience is carried through across most of the games on the site. For example, when users pick the "Horton Hears a Tune" game from Horton the elephant's list of activities, they can compose their own melody on the groovy organ-like instrument under the supportive eyes of Horton himself. Then, in true social fashion, they can save their tune and share it with family and friends.

FIGURE 5.3

"Horton Hears a Tune" lets kids compose music and share it.

Make Learning Part of the Game

As a designer, you know that providing help when and where your users need it works better than forcing them to leave the task they're trying to complete to get help. This is especially true for 4–6-year-olds, who have a strong curiosity for why things are the way they are and want to know everything *right away*. Unlike the "school stinks" mentality of earlier generations, today's kids are fascinated with learning and want to soak up as much information as possible.

This new attitude could be because learning is more dynamic, more hands-on, and more inventive than it's been in the past, or because computers, tablets, and other digital teaching tools make learning fun. However, younger kids still lack patience when learning takes longer than they'd like. You'll want to provide short, manageable instructions to make learning fast, easy, and pleasurable, and to incorporate learning into the experience itself.

The *Dinosaur Chess* app does a great job with structured teaching, as well as on-the-spot assistance to help kids learn how to play chess (see Figure 5.4). Upon launching the app, children get to choose what they want to do. The great thing about *Dinosaur Chess* is that it's not just all about chess—kids can take lessons, check their overall progress, and even participate in a "dino fight!"

One perk is how the app links the activities via a treasure-hunt-style map on the menu screen. It gently recommends a progression through the activities (which older kids will follow), but is subtle enough to allow exploration. This feature is great for kids who like to break the rules, because it establishes a flow, yet invites users to deviate from it in a subtle yet effective way.

FIGURE 5.4
Dinosaur Chess offers many opportunities for learning.

When users select the "learn" option, they are taken to a screen where an avuncular dinosaur (who, for some reason, is Scottish) talks kids through the mechanics of chess in a non-intimidating way. Since these kids are still learning to read, the designers used voice-overs instead of text, which works really well here.

The lessons are broken up into short, manageable chunks—essential for learning via listening—which let the 4–6s learn a little at a time and progress when they are ready. The children can also try out various moves after learning them, which is particularly effective with younger users who learn by seeing and doing (see Figure 5.5).

If this app were designed for an adult audience, the lessons would be a little longer and would probably include text explanations in addition to the audio, since a combination of listening and reading works best for grown-ups. However, the brief audio segments coupled with animated examples are perfect for younger users' short attention spans and desire to learn as much as quickly as possible.

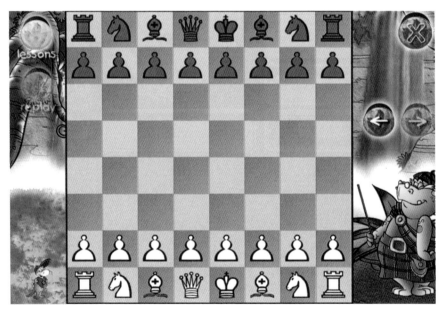

FIGURE 5.5
Dinosaur Chess teaches kids how to play chess in short, informational chunks.

My favorite aspect of *Dinosaur Chess* is its guided playing. At any point during the game, kids can press the "?" button for help. Instead of popping a layer, which many sites and apps do (even those designed for a younger audience), *Dinosaur Chess* uses subtle animation and voice-overs to show the users what their next moves should be, as shown in Figure 5.6.

FIGURE 5.6
Dinosaur Chess uses animation and voice-overs to provide contextual help.

TIP DON'T DUMB IT DOWN

When creating an experience for this age group, don't fall into the trap of "dumbing down" your design. These kids are more sophisticated than they may appear initially. They're capable of solving relatively complex problems, they're able to mentally categorize quite efficiently, they've got a decent-sized vocabulary, and they're technologically savvy. Although they may gravitate toward games designed for younger kids, they're ready for more complicated interactions.

Give Feedback and Reinforcement

As anyone knows who has dealt with this age group, 4–6-year-olds have short attention spans. This is particularly true of the younger ones, because kids ages 6 and up are able to pay attention for longer periods of time and absorb more information in a single session. What's interesting (and challenging) about these younger ones is that they get frustrated at *themselves* for not being able to focus, and then they channel that frustration onto the experience.

A common response to this from designers is: "Well, I'll make my app/game/site super fun and interesting so that kids will want to play longer." That's not going to happen. A better approach is to identify opportunities within the experience to provide feedback, in order to encourage kids to continue.

Here are some ways to keep children focused on a particular activity:

- **Limit distractions.** With a child audience, designers tend to want to make everything on the screen do something, but if you want your 4–6s to complete a task (for example, finish a puzzle or play a game), then remove extra functionality.

- **Break it up.** As when you're designing for 2-4s, it's best to break activities for 4–6s into manageable components. The components can be a bit bigger than ones you might design for a younger audience, but many clear, simple steps are better than fewer, longer ones. While adult users prefer to complete as few steps as possible, and scroll down to finish a task on a screen, 4–6s like finishing a step and moving to a new screen.

- **Make it rewarding.** Provide feedback after each piece of an activity is completed, which will help your users stay motivated to continue. If you have the time and budget, use a combination of feedback mechanisms, to keep an element of surprise and discovery in the task-completion process.

Starting at around age 4, kids understand what it means to "win," and they become quite anxious at the prospect of "losing." In the late 1980s, parents and educators decided it would be a good idea to put off the concept of losing until much later, so they stopped keeping score during weekend sports and enforced "ties" in games and competitions. Unfortunately, in many cases, this strategy backfired when the kids, who are now young adults, stopped "winning" (for example, didn't get into the college of their choice, or didn't get the job they wanted)—because they now had a very hard time getting motivated to try again.

The problem is, as adults, we're too focused on "losing" as a negative experience, and we channel that onto kids. If we make losing "okay," and even think about ways to turn it into a learning opportunity, our kids will be much better off than if we continue to pretend that it doesn't exist.

Some ideas for making losing, or being wrong, in a digital experience more interesting are the following:

- Play a funny sound (think "sad trombone").

- Show a short, funny animation.

- Create a very simple "runner-up" game, like an easy multiple-choice question.

- Show the child what he did well.

Most importantly, always, always provide the opportunity to try again. Kids respond really well to the idea of "I'll do better next time."

Keep It Free-Form

The 4–6-age bracket gravitates toward activities that are open and free-form, with simple, basic rules (and lots of opportunities to deviate from the rules). This changes pretty dramatically when kids hit age 7 or so. At that point, they become quite focused on staying within boundaries and need a certain level of structure in order to feel comfortable. However, these younger kids like to break the rules and test limits, and digital environments are the perfect places to do this.

Zoopz.com has a great mosaic-maker tool, which lets kids enhance existing mosaic designs or create their own from scratch (see Figures 5.7 and 5.8).

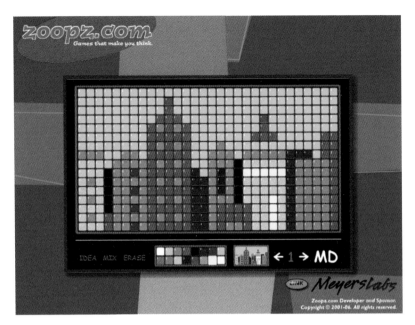

FIGURE 5.7
An existing mosaic design from *Zoopz.com*, which lets kids experiment and test limits.

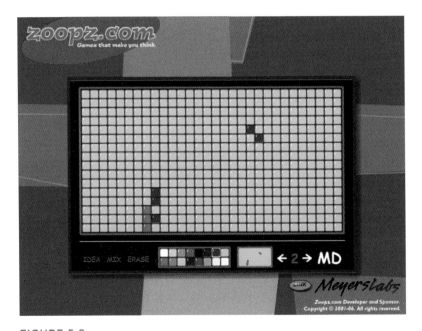

FIGURE 5.8
Zoopz.com mosaic-creator enables kids to create their own cool designs.

The nice thing about *Zoopz* is that it requires little to no explanation in order to make mosaics—kids can jump right in and start playing. This feature is important, as younger ones will get frustrated if they need to listen to detailed instructions before getting started and will likely move on to something else before the instructions are complete. Typically, 4- and 5-year-olds will leave websites and close apps that they can't immediately figure out. Older kids will hang around and pay attention to directions if the perceived reward is high enough, but young ones abandon the site right away. So if your game allows for free exploration, make sure that it's really free and doesn't require lots of information in order to play.

An important thing to note about open exploration/creation: If you're designing something with a "takeaway," as *Zoopz* is, make sure that kids can either print or save their creations. The only thing kids like better than playing by their own rules is showing their work to others. *Zoopz* misses an opportunity here, because it doesn't offer the ability for kids to share their work, or print it out to show to friends and family. This feature becomes even more important as kids get older. We'll talk at length about sharing, saving, and storing in Chapter 6, "Kid 6–8: The Big Kids."

Keep It Challenging

The worst insult from a child between the ages of 4 and 5 is to call something "babyish." They're part of the big-kid crowd now, and the last thing they want is to feel like they're using a site or playing a game that's meant for younger kids. Unfortunately, it's hard to pin down exactly what "babyish" means, because the definition changes from kid to kid, but in my experience, children call something "babyish" when it's not difficult or challenging enough for them. Since kids show increased memory function (and more sophisticated motor skills) starting at around age 4, adding multiple steps to games and activities helps keep them on their toes.

As designers, we instinctively want to make stuff that users can master immediately. If you're designing for elementary-school kids, you'll want to move away from that mindset. While it's true that children need to be able to easily *figure out* the objectives of a game or app right away, they don't necessarily have to do it *perfectly* the first time. Instead, build in easier layers early on so that kids can complete them quickly, but throw in some extras that might be a little harder for them. For example, if you're designing a game where kids have to shoot at flying objects, send in a super-fast projectile they have to catch to win extra points or add a harder "bonus round." Kids will be less likely to call something "babyish" if it takes them several tries to master. And they'll appreciate the vote of confidence you're giving to their memory and agility.

PARENTS ARE USERS, TOO

When adding complexity to your game or app, you'll still need to make the basic premise simple and clear. A little parental intervention is sometimes necessary, in order to explain rules and demonstrate interactions, but when parents or siblings have to become very involved in game mechanics, it's frustrating for all parties.

Try not to place too much emphasis on "winning" and keep the perceived "rewards" small and unexciting, if you have them at all. Kids tend to ask parents to step in and help with the trickier parts if the reward for winning is really high. While I believe that a parent should be in the room when kids are online and should check on kids frequently when they're using a device, too much involvement takes away some autonomy from the kids and prevents them from learning as much as they could and should.

Chapter Checklist

Here's a checklist for designing for 4–6-year-olds.

Does your design cover the following areas?

- ☐ Feel "social"?
- ☐ Break up instructions and progression into manageable chunks?
- ☐ Provide immediate positive feedback after each small milestone?
- ☐ Allow for invention and self-expression?
- ☐ Include multi-step activities to leverage improved memory function?

In the next chapter, we'll see some bigger changes in how children relate to technology and the design challenges that come with those changes.

Favorite App: *Endless Alphabet*

When I asked Samantha to show me her favorite app, she skipped right over all the Disney Princess apps on her mother's phone and went right to *Endless Alphabet* (see Figure 5.9). This fantastic little game lets kids use animated letter creatures to spell interesting words like *nibble, pester,* and *zigzag*. The app reads the word, gives a definition, and then lets the user drag the letter characters to their place within the word. As the child drags the letter, it makes its signature sound in a funny voice; for example, when the letter *A* is tapped, it goes "ah ah ah ah AH!" in a funny little-girl voice. The app also shows an animation of the word and its meaning (see Figure 5.10.)

I asked Samantha what she liked best about *Endless Alphabet*. She said, "I love that I get to pick the words I want to do. I don't have to go in order like ABCDE." This reinforces what we know about 4–6-year-olds: They like a little structure, but enjoy the freedom to choose their own direction and discover the app's functions independently as they explore. Samantha also liked "the letter guys' funny voices" and the way the letters "squiggle and jump when

FIGURE 5.9
Endless Alphabet lets kids play with letters and words.

you drag them." This immediate feedback and delightful little lagniappe of the animated letters helped engage Samantha in the app and highlight the learning it was designed to provide.

What she liked least about *Endless Alphabet* was that (with the free version), there are only a limited number of words to choose from. "I want some new words!" Samantha said. "I've done *vegetable* like a hundred times already!" Samantha's mother will most likely splurge and pay the $5.99 for the full app, since Samantha can now recognize words "in real life" like *tangle, multiply,* and *sticky,* and her interest in letters and reading has increased.

The main themes I noticed while observing Samantha and asking her questions were exploration, surprise, response, and self-direction. I was also really interested to note that she recognized the fact that she was learning, and that she thought that was really cool. "This is a fun game, but it also teaches me. I already know all the letters. This shows me how they make words together and how I can make words and learn new ones. I love it!"

FIGURE 5.10

Through sound, animation, and imagery, *Endless Alphabet* shows kids the meaning of words instead of just telling them.

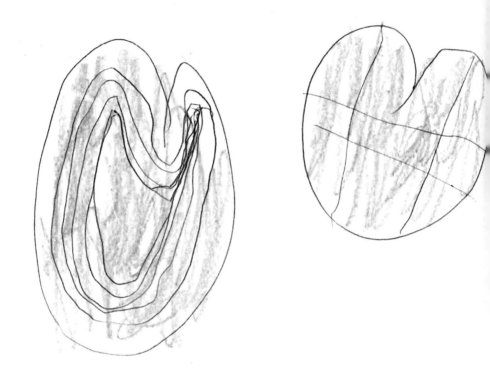
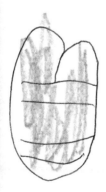
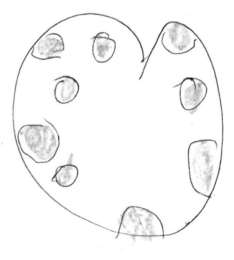

CHAPTER 6

Kids 6-8: The Big Kids

Lilly, Age 6

Only a child sees things with perfect clarity, because it hasn't developed all those filters which prevent us from seeing things that we don't expect to see.

—Douglas Adams

I love designing for 6–8s best of all. Why? Because they're introspective, complex, conniving, and open-minded, and still get incredibly excited by stuff they think is cool. They haven't developed the healthy cynicism that comes at around age 10; they're years away from 'tween angst; they still like their stuffed animals; and they can read. They are the perfect combination of sophistication and innocence.

Who Are They?

You'll have lots of chances to experiment when designing for these kids. Keep in mind, though, this is the age when kids start becoming influenced by what their peers do instead of what the adults in their lives do. That brings a whole new set of challenges, as shown in the characteristics highlighted in Table 6.1.

Outside Influences

When they start elementary school, children's sphere of influence expands from that of their family and closest friends to include peers, teachers, coaches, and others. This experience helps them see objects, behaviors, and situations in different ways and from different perspectives. This additional awareness, coupled with an increased ability to pay closer attention to what's going on around them, causes them to feel a little out of control. As a result, they look for situations they can master and orchestrate.

Let's go through each facet in Table 6.1 and see what they mean when designing for kids in this age group.

Leveling Up

Kids from 6–8 have a much easier time focusing on tasks than they did when they were 4, just a few short years ago. This focus sometimes turns into a little bit of an obsession—kids will work on a particular task over and over again until they've mastered it. When designing

TABLE 6.1 CONSIDERATIONS FOR 6–8-YEAR-OLDS

6–8-year-olds…	This means that…	You'll want to…
Are very focused.	They like to master something completely before moving on.	Incorporate concepts of progression, "leveling up," and continued achievement.
Prefer up-front knowledge to exploratory investigation.	They don't like guesswork. They'll be less likely to explore and more likely to ask "What am I supposed to do here?"	Be very clear at the beginning of the experience what the point is, what the kids will be doing, and why.
Understand and appreciate the idea of permanence.	They want to be able to return to an experience at any time and continue where they left off.	Allow kids to save, store, and share the things they do. Create tie-ins between virtual experiences and physical ones.
Feel a little out of control about the world around them.	They're very focused on following the rules, and craft elaborate guidelines for themselves and their behavior.	Create a set of clear, easy-to-follow rules for them, but let them interpret and expand on these.
Prefer quantity to quality.	They like experiences that allow them to gather and collect, instead of simply excel.	Incorporate basic gamification strategies (awards, badges, and so on) that they can earn and stockpile.
Are starting to feel scared, suspicious, and distrustful of those they don't know.	They're beginning to be hesitant about meeting new people and trying new things.	Back away from social interactions and focus more on self-expression.

for these kids, you can help support this focus by providing multiple levels of accomplishment, even if you're not designing a game, per se.

For games, you should make the first few levels pretty easy to ace. Increase the difficulty, but give kids the feeling of accomplishment and mastery early on. As the levels go up, naturally, you'll make them more difficult, but keep the delta between levels pretty consistent.

For educational sites and apps, it's best to establish patterns of progression early on, so kids know the mechanics of what they need to do on each screen before they get there. This pattern lets them anticipate what they'll come up against as they move through the interface. For example, when designing an interface to teach math, keep the general layout of the math problems the same across screens, but just increase the difficulty of the problems. You can change stuff like colors, icons, and animations on each screen, but make the basic structure consistent so that kids can feel a sense of comfort and familiarity. If users feel like they might not be able to accomplish something at first glance, they'll be less likely to engage.

PBS Kids Go! offers a wide variety of games geared toward kids from 2–10, but 6–8s are their sweet spot. Because the developers are committed to building collaborative learning relationships with children, they make sure to feature games that can grow with the kids they're trying to reach. Most of the games on the site, as well as their individual apps, start off with pretty general, easy-to-grasp activities and then get progressively more difficult as the kids are able to master them.

For example, the *Fizzy's Lunch Lab Freestyle Fizz* game lets kids collect healthy foods like cheese, bread, and apples while avoiding French fries, hot dogs, and chocolate bars (see Figure 6.1). The game starts off relatively easy, letting users get used to the controls and figure out the best way to move around to collect the foods, but as kids level up, the game gets harder, with more items to collect and more to avoid.

FIGURE 6.1
Fizzy's Lunch Lab lets kids level up in interesting ways.

Explain, Explain, and Explain Again

While younger children prefer to explore and learn as they go, 6–8s want all the information up front, to make sure they get it right the first time. Starting at age 6, opinions of others become super-important to kids, even if that "other" is a digital interface. They don't want the game, or app, or device to think they're dumb or unsophisticated. Having all the rules established before they begin makes these kids feel better prepared to excel.

It's important to note, though, that if you find your interface requires a lot of explanation—say, more than a couple of short sentences—it's probably too complicated and will likely turn kids away. These youngsters have just started to read, and if the directions make the experience sound too difficult, they won't want to participate.

Of course, the best interfaces are those requiring little to no explanation, where kids can figure out what to do without reading instructions. So, similar to designing for adults, try to make the experience easy to figure out. Don't use copy as a crutch for a confusing interface.

Poptropica, a virtual world where kids can create their own characters and engage in collaborative play with others, offers a very simple sign-up process that gets kids ready to start using the environment (see Figure 6.2). Although this process is broken up into several steps, it gives users a chance to fully understand what they need to do along the way and sets them up for success. While adults prefer to move through tasks quickly, 6–8s are more concerned with doing the task in the right way, so a greater number of clearly outlined steps works better for them.

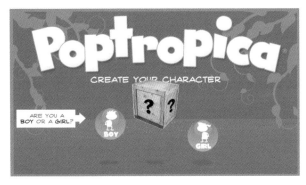

FIGURE 6.2
Poptropica uses clear, visual explanations to help kids complete the registration process.

Contrast this with LEGO Creator's *Builder's Island*, an interesting and exploratory game, which lets kids build structures in a virtual world (see Figure 6.3). LEGO offers no instructions, just an overhead view of an island where kids are supposed to build. The interface isn't very easy to figure out, and there are few instructions to guide children through the game. There isn't even a place where kids can click to get more information.

This will pose a bit of a problem for 6–8-year-olds, who like to have all the facts before they begin using a site or an app. No matter how interesting a game looks, if they feel there is even a slight chance that they'll mess up or get something wrong, these kids will be less likely to engage. So 8–10-year-olds, who consider themselves experts, will probably be undaunted by the lack of instructions here, but 6–8s will struggle. We'll look at this in more detail in Chapter 7, "Kids 8–10: The 'Cool' Factor."

FIGURE 6.3
LEGO Creator does not provide explanations or information on how to play, which will make 6–8-year-olds very uncomfortable.

Saving, Storing, Sharing, and Collecting

Children are able to grasp the concept of "permanence" at a pretty early age. If you move a toddler's toy from in front of the couch to behind the couch, she'll know that the object still exists, but it's just hidden from view. What's missing from the toddler perspective, however, is the idea of continuity—if a toy is behind the couch when you leave the room, it will still be behind the couch when you come back to the room, not in the toy box where it usually is. Kids figure out the continuity concept at around age 3, but they're not able to apply it to intangible ideas or situations until they turn 6. For example, a 4-year-old will expect a movie or TV show to start from the beginning when he turns it on, while an older child will expect it to pick up where he left off. In fact, this older child will become distressed if the movie does *not* start up from the point at which he turned it off.

So, how can you reinforce this continuity in a digital environment? By allowing children to save and store their accomplishments within the experience and letting them easily resume play from the exact point where they left off. *Webkinz*, a virtual world where kids take care of digital pets, does this really well.

In *Webkinz*, kids collect and care for virtual pets. (These have an offline component too, which we'll discuss shortly.) They build houses, which they can then furnish and decorate, for their pets, and can take their pets on adventures to play games and compete in contests. There are also a few "daily" activities, which kids can only play once a day, allowing them to collect rewards and "kinzcash," which they can use to buy stuff for their pets.

The great thing about *Webkinz* is that it returns users to where they were when they last logged off. If they logged off from a room in their virtual house, they are returned to that same room. If they logged off from a game, they return to the game. *Webkinz* also reinforces the concept of continuity in how it treats the pets. If a pet was wearing a baseball hat when the user logged off, that pet will still be wearing the same hat when the user logs back on. This concept of permanence is both rewarding and comforting to kids 6–8. In a world where they feel increasingly out of control, it's nice to have a consistent place to return to, where they can be assured that things will be just as they left them.

NOTE HISTORY OF *WEBKINZ*

Webkinz is one of the oldest and best virtual worlds for kids. Ganz, a Canadian toy company specializing in stuffed animals and collectible toys, launched the site in April 2005 to enormous fanfare. While its popularity has waned in recent years due to competitors in the space, it still sees about 3 million unique visitors each month. In 2009, *Business Insider* estimated *Webkinz* revenue to be about $750 million annually.

Webkinz's daily activities also help with permanence and continuity. In the daily *Gem Hunt* game, kids dig in virtual caves for gems they can collect to complete their "Crown of Wonder" (see Figure 6.4). They can only go on a gem hunt once a day, which both increases the desirability of the activity and the consistency of play, but they can look at their collection of gems whenever they want. This concept, of a growing virtual collection, is very attractive to kids and results in a significant increase in daily site visits.

Another way that *Webkinz* furthers the ideas of permanence and continuity is by selling a complete line of stuffed animals to match the pets in the virtual world. In fact, kids must have an animal and an entry code in order to start using the site at all. When kids sign up online, using the entry code that comes with their stuffed animal, a virtual representation of their toy appears on screen, which they can then use to play games, dress up, and care for in the environment. Having a physical connection to a virtual entity is amazingly compelling to 6–8s. It's a consistent reminder to log in to the site, but it also extends the concepts communicated in the virtual world. Kids can collect both the stuffed animals and the virtual pets and build their own communities.

TIP TAKE-AWAYS ADD INTEREST

The 6–8s love having physical reminders of what they do in a digital space. A great way to provide this connection between the virtual and the physical is to create printable certificates, badges, and awards for kids to download and collect.

FIGURE 6.4

Webkinz reinforces permanence and continuity in its daily gem hunt.

High Scores

The ability to save and share high scores or achievements in a digital environment is exciting to children, too. Not only does this let them chart their progress, but it also gives them tangible goals to work toward. For example, if kids set a personal goal to spell 100 words right in a spelling game, they can continue to work toward that goal in a cumulative fashion and see where they improve instead of starting from scratch each time.

Let's take a look at *DigitZ*, a tetris-like math game for iOS. The great thing about *DigitZ* is that it lets kids go back and see their score for every level of the game they've completed, from the easiest to the hardest (see Figure 6.5). In fact, the two main calls-to-action on the landing screen are to play the game and to view their high scores.

This ability to see scores right away allows children to chart their progress, lends permanence and flow to the game itself, and motivates them to continue to excel. Establishing these goals at the outset of the game and being transparent about what kids are working toward helps keep the momentum going and inspires continued play.

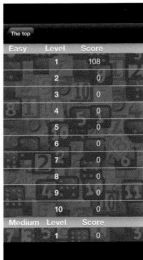

FIGURE 6.5
DigitZ lets kids see their scores easily.

Sharing

The wonderful *Storybird* site is great for kids of all ages, but 6–8s will especially love it because of the way it lets them use their newfound storytelling and deductive reasoning skills. *Storybird* has mastered the art of letting kids share stories in a safe, yet meaningful way. As per the site, "*Storybird* reverses visual storytelling by starting with the images and 'unlocking' the story inside." It lets kids make up their own stories by first choosing a series of illustrations from a huge repository of images and then crafting tales around these images (see Figure 6.6).

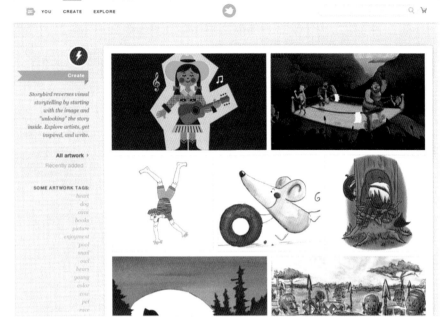

FIGURE 6.6

Storybird lets kids choose image collections and craft stories around the images.

In school, students "write" stories first and then illustrate them after they have the basic narrative down. *Storybird* lets children turn the process inside out, by using images to spark ideas and letting the kids develop the ideas from there.

Storybird has an ecommerce component, where parents can purchase printed versions of the stories their children create. I'm not normally a fan of kids' sites that encourage the purchasing of products from within the experience, but the permanence and tangibility of the *Storybird* books create a robust all-around experience for the 6–8-year-olds. Kids can also write stories and post them on the site, for others to read and enjoy, free of charge.

After kids select the collection of images they want to use, they are guided through the "writing" process via a simple, clear, representational interface that lets them watch the book evolve as they create it, as shown in Figure 6.7. Younger children may need parents to help them enter the text, but early readers will be able to jump right in and start writing.

FIGURE 6.7

Storybird's clean interface allows kids to focus on being creative without getting in the way of that creativity.

Playing by the Rules

I did an observational study with some second-graders a few years back, where I got to watch groups of friends play together. I took them into a separate room with no toys or books, and asked them to play while I got my "papers" together. Most of the groups decided to play rock band (which is evidently this latest generation's answer to "house"). The most fascinating aspect of this free-play activity was that the groups spent most of the time coming up with roles and rules instead of actually engaging in the role-play. They first decided who everyone on the group was going to "be." As is typical with second-graders, one kid stepped up as the leader and started assigning roles. When she told one little girl that she'd be the drummer, the little girl said, "I don't want to be the drummer; I want to be a veterinarian."

The game came to a screeching halt. After all, there aren't too many veterinarians in rock bands these days.

Kids start really focusing in on rules at around age 7. They are beginning to see how big the world really is, and the concept of rules—to govern behavior, interactions, and communication—is extremely comforting to them. They develop elaborate rules for how they play, talk, and generally conduct themselves. And they hold others in their social sphere to these same rules.

This presents really interesting implications when designing virtual environments. We know kids like rules, but when the rules for a game become too limiting or too difficult to follow, they'll find something else to do. The trick is to develop a clear set of rules that are easy to understand and follow, but flexible enough for kids to make their own. This is easier for games with specific objectives, and it's more difficult for environments that rely on exploration and self-expression.

Let's take a look at what the folks at *Club Penguin* are doing.

Club Penguin is a virtual world for kids and adults (see Figure 6.8). It lets kids create penguin avatars and move through a virtual arctic environment where they can play games, chat, and build their own igloos. The *Club Penguin* creators developed a robust yet flexible set of rules that help kids (and parents) feel comfortable moving through the interface.

FIGURE 6.8
Club Penguin's rules are both easy to follow and flexible.

Rules Create Comfort, but Can Get in the Way

During a usability test last year, 7-year-old Georgie came into the lab looking dejected, giving me one-word answers and seeming less than excited about the apps we were researching. I asked her if everything was okay, and she said, "I got some dirt on my new shoes." I asked her to show me, and sure enough, there was a streak of brown dirt on what looked like new white Mary Janes. As a new parent, I had a ton of baby wipes in my bag, so I pulled one out and wiped off the offending mark. Color flooded back into Georgie's cheeks, and she became suddenly very interested in playing on the iPad.

"I'm glad we got your shoe clean, Georgie," I said. "Would your mom have been mad at you if she saw the dirt?" Georgie's mother was a work colleague of mine. In fact, she was down the hall, having coffee with the other participants' parents during this test. She seemed like a pretty reasonable, engaged parent, but it's hard to tell what sets people off. (We've since become friends, and she gave me permission to use this example.)

Georgie looked at me like I was crazy. "Oh, no," she said. "My mom says shoes are supposed to get dirty. But I would have been mad at myself."

Georgie had created her own set of internal guidelines for how she was supposed to behave. Evidently, keeping new shoes clean was among these guidelines. When you're designing environments for kids, they'll follow your rules to the letter. So you'll want to make sure that the rules you create are flexible enough to follow closely, while still allowing for a level of interpretation.

The great thing about *Club Penguin's* rules is that, although they cover some serious business, they're written to support free play and focus on safety and community. This application gives kids and parents a sense of comfort and control within the space, while at the same time encouraging them to have fun. The image of the penguins high-fiving each other reinforces the sense of community that the creators are trying to convey.

This concept of flexible rules may seem to be at odds with what we discussed earlier about providing clear, concrete explanations. The difference here is, rules provide global structure to an overall interface, while instructions provide specific information about individual components. The former needs to be elastic and allow for some interpretation, while the latter needs to be detailed enough to ensure success and accomplishment.

So what happened with our rock band? The young ringleader, who struggled with the idea of a veterinarian in the midst of her musicians, was able to bend her rules to create a compromise. "Well…you can be the VETERINARIAN drummer!" The aspiring veterinarian was happy, the leader was happy, and the other players were comforted at the possibility that one could be both a veterinarian and a drummer at the same time.

> **TIP** MAKING THE RULES
>
> Make sure that the rules you create for your site or app are clear and easy for children to follow with little to no interpretation. An example of a well-constructed rule might be: "When writing a story, try to use pictures and words that are positive and respectful." A poorly constructed rule would say: "Don't curse or use words that could be considered offensive, dirty, or insulting in your stories."

We Need Some Stinkin' Badges

It's true that 6–8s love to gather and collect stuff. When my brother was about 7, he started collecting mini soaps from hotels. Whenever we went on a family vacation, he would take a couple of soaps from the bathroom, wrap them in tissues, and place them carefully in a special toiletry bag. These not only served as physical reminders of our trips, but also let him accumulate "proof" of all the places he'd been, almost like stamps in a passport. This type of collecting is equally important in a digital space, for both kids and adults.

Let's think about the implications of this concept on behavior modification. If you're consistently rewarded for positive behavior, for example, exercise, smoking cessation, losing weight, you'll be more likely to continue this behavior. This is true for kids, too. When kids associate behavior with positive outcomes, it fosters the desired behavior. If you want kids to do certain things within your interface, give them cool stuff for doing it. This behavior-reward system is the basis of "gamification."

Unfortunately, "gamification" has almost become a pejorative term for designers. It conjures up images of false accolades, meaningless rewards for common behaviors, and unimportant milestones to share via social networks. When it comes to designing for kids, however, the concept of gamification is very powerful. It's digital proof of all the cool stuff they do online.

Fortunately, it's easy to do this well. First, identify the key behaviors you want to reward within the experience you're designing, and then identify a simple way for kids to accumulate stuff for doing them.

When I was working on *Planet Orange,* a virtual world designed to teach children financial literacy, we wanted to include something that would serve as an impetus for kids to complete all the activities on the site. We created a series of badges that users would earn after finishing the projects on each continent on the "planet" (see Figure 6.9). We also created printable certificates that kids could hang up to celebrate their accomplishments.

While our ideas were founded on the correct principles, we over-complicated the rewards model. Since the site was about money, we created a complex currency structure, in addition to the badges, where kids could earn "money" to buy stuff for their personal space stations and astronaut avatars (see Figure 6.10). The problem was, we were rewarding the same behaviors with both badges and currency. So we essentially diluted the importance of both badges and money—called "o-bux"—resulting in the devaluation of the activities on the site. Lesson here: Too many rewards for similar behaviors makes the reward structure become meaningless. Collecting items is an effective way to learn, but only if you're collecting stuff that reinforces the ideas you're learning.

Bottom line: Using badges and awards to encourage site use is compelling for kids. Just make sure that the awards you give support the right behaviors in the right way.

FIGURE 6.9
Planet Orange awards badges for completing activities.

FIGURE 6.10

Planet Orange also provides currency rewards for completing the same activities.

Stranger Danger

By the time children reach the age of 4, they've been more than adequately warned about the perils of talking to strangers. In fact, many of them are quite frightened at the prospect of being around strangers, let alone talking to them. This fear continues to grow as kids get older and wiser about the ways of the world. However, a normal healthy fear about encountering strangers in the real world can turn into abject terror when dealing with the notion of strangers in digital space. This is because anyone can be a stranger, even someone who seems to be a regular kid just like them. There is no real way to know if the person you're talking to online is 8 or 80, and that lack of control and knowledge can be truly terrifying to a child. This "stranger danger" fear presents implications when designing for this audience, because if the experience you're designing has a large social component, kids will be less likely to engage.

As the power of technology continues to evolve, many companies want to inject a social element into their kids' experiences, simply because the ability is there. It's true that collaborative learning and exploration works really well with children, but only if this collaboration can be done anonymously. To most kids, "social" means saying hello to folks in the hallway, not interacting with them online.

It's possible to design for meaningful online engagement with a child audience, but you *have* to proceed with caution. For example, crafting a robust set of rules around interaction, as *Club Penguin* does, helps kids and parents feel more comfortable in a given space. You can also leverage "canned" messages for kids to send to each other, to foster communication without real free-form interaction.

The people at *Webkinz* also do a nice job with "canned chat" (see Figure 6.11). Kids can pick from a set of preselected topics and choose pretyped messages, called *KinzChat*, to communicate with others in the virtual world.

FIGURE 6.11
Webkinz lets kids message each other, but only via canned chat.

However, children cannot type in free-form messages to each other at *Webkinz*, thereby eliminating the possibility of inappropriate or predatory interactions. This structure helps kids feel more comfortable in an interactive environment without worrying that a stranger will start up a conversation.

Other sites, including *Club Penguin*, let parents pick the level of interaction they want their kids to have with others. Part of this is due to COPPA regulations (see the interview with Linnette Attai at the end of this chapter), but part of it is based on a conscious design decision to help kids feel safe. *Club Penguin* offers levels of use, which range from no chat mechanism at all through full free-text messaging. The 6–8s tend to prefer the middle ground, which gives them the opportunity to communicate in a limited capacity with pre-existing messages.

Designing Canned Chat

When designing a canned chat experience, make sure that the topics are varied enough to appeal to children's different interests, but not so broad as to be confusing. Additionally, make sure that the phrases you allow kids to use are easily understood. Use short words and sentences, and reflect the nature of the experience you're designing.

An effective use of canned chat is to develop a series of questions that kids can ask each other and provide appropriate responses for kids to use to reply. For example, a question like "What's your favorite animal?" is a great way for kids to open up conversations online in a non-threatening way, become comfortable with the idea of communicating, and share information about themselves. The answers you provide for them to use should range from safe to exciting, and should let the kids feel some element of self-expression. For example "cat," "dog," "monkey," "elephant," and "wooly mammoth" represent a good range of options. Limit the options within each category to five and under, as kids have difficulty choosing from lots of different selections.

Most likely, you won't be able to craft a broad enough set of generic messages to use all the time. So what you can do is offer different message types based on context. For example, if your experience allows kids to compete in a game, push messages like "nice shot!" "way to go!" and "let's play again." If you're encouraging kids to communicate in a creative or building environment, messages like "great idea!" "nice picture!" and "cool design!" let kids comment on each other's work. For 6–8s, you'll want to avoid negative messaging, and you may even want to stay away from neutral messaging (for example, phrases like "not bad") since kids aren't great at interpreting meaning. When they get older, and become a little more experienced at context and subtext, you can weave in more constructive messages.

The Anonymity Factor

There are problems other than the children's comfort level in offering open chat communication. The concept of anonymity is extremely seductive to people of all ages. Think about it—if you could say anything you wanted to anyone you wanted and no one would know it was you, what would you say? It's hard for adults to control what they say under the guise of anonymity, and it's even more difficult for kids.

Especially kids who are learning new naughty words almost daily. In addition, the idea of "Internet predators" has taken on a life of its own. While it's highly unlikely that a real predator will approach a child in your digital environment, there are plenty of creepy people out there who will say creepy things. You want to limit the opportunity for the creepy to come out in the experience you create.

When researching for an article a year or so ago, I signed up for an account on the *Barbie Girls* site (which has since been shut down). I signed up for the most "permissive" account, giving me full access to view and create free-form messages. Almost immediately, another "girl" approached me, and began asking extremely suggestive questions, about what I was wearing and whom I was with. I played along for a little while, to see how far this person would go, until I decided to report her (him?) to the site moderators, who promptly blocked her. As an adult, I was able to quickly assess the situation and report the creepy person, but for an 8-year-old who really, really wants to be liked, it might not be so clear-cut.

Other good ways to foster communication in a safe and positive manner are to allow children to post stuff that they've created and allow other kids to comment on it, using canned chat, or "stickers," or badges. The 6–8s love to express themselves and share their thoughts and ideas, so it's a good idea to create an outlet for that, even for something as simple as showing their high scores.

PARENTS ARE USERS, TOO

When you're designing an experience for kids, it's always good to have a section for parents. Even if you don't use any communication tools or collect any personal data, you'll still want to let parents and adults know a little bit about your environment: what the goals are, what you hope kids will come away with, and so on. Parents will be more likely to let a child use or download a site or an app if they understand what it's for and how it will be used. You also may want parents to play a role in helping their kids get the most from the experience. For example, usage tools and tips for adults can help encourage adoption and engagement.

Chapter Checklist

If you get the opportunity to design for a 6–8-year-old audience, I encourage you to take it. It will be a blast, and you'll learn a lot from these savvy little customers. When designing for this crew, answer the following questions.

Does your design cover the following areas?

- [ ] Feature progression and "leveling up"?
- [ ] Clearly show the goals and purpose of the experience at the beginning?
- [ ] Let kids save, store, and share their progress?
- [ ] Offer a set of clear and easy rules, yet provide opportunities to interpret and expand on these?
- [ ] Allow kids to earn and collect badges and awards?
- [ ] Focus on self-expression instead of social interaction?

Interestingly, 6–8-year-olds have more in common in terms of attitude and behavior with 10–12s than they do with 8–10s. When we dive into how to design for 8–10-year-olds in the next chapter, you'll see how they represent their own unique little pocket of awesome.

Favorite App: *Mega Run*

Andy's parents don't hand over their phones for him to play with all that often, but when they do, he watches YouTube videos and plays *Mega Run*. "It's a really cool game where you get to run and jump and climb over obstacles and stuff. You jump over animals and sticks." *Mega Run* actually has a loose narrative associated with it—a little monster has to rescue his kidnapped brother and sister—but Andy, like a typical 6-year-old, all but ignored the story and focused on the mechanics of the game itself.

When I asked him what the best part of the game was, he said, "The best part is you can pick your own person. If you get enough points, you can change your person. I like the blue penguin." A little more probing revealed that users can, in fact, switch out their player after accruing enough points. I asked Andy to show me how it worked. Sure enough, after he finished playing a round, he was able to open a layer with a bunch of different characters on it, each with an associated points value and some with a lock icon next to them.

"There are 10 people. I need 3 more. So you have to get enough points. You don't get a person every time, but when you do, they put a person up on the screen. Then there are different buttons to push. You push a button, and all the people come up, but some you can't choose because you don't have enough points. When you choose a new person, you give up some of your points," Andy said, beautifully describing the app's implementation of virtual currency and leveling up (see Figure 6.12). He showed me all the characters he had amassed and demonstrated how he could switch them out when he felt like playing with a new one.

Andy loved playing the game itself, but took special pride in telling me about his points and his characters. Like most 6–8s, he liked the permanence of these objects and what they meant to him in terms of his own achievement within the game.

The themes that surfaced during my interview with Andy included progression, achievement, permanence, and collection. As much as he enjoyed the challenges presented in the game itself, it was the collecting and leveling up that made the experience all the more rewarding.

FIGURE 6.12

Kids can level up by trading points for new characters in *Mega Run*.

Linnette Attai

President and Founder, PlayWell LLC

Linnette Attai is a media and marketing compliance executive with extensive expertise navigating regulatory and self-regulatory environments surrounding advertising, marketing, content, privacy, safety, and ethical concerns. Since 2000, her primary area of focus has been the multi-billion dollar children's entertainment industry, including the special considerations faced by digital, mobile, consumer product, food, movie, toy, video game, and television companies creating content and marketing intended for children and teens.

Linnette is the founder of PlayWell, LLC, a consulting firm focused on guiding clients through compliance concerns related to media and marketing, including digital and mobile privacy and safety concerns. She also serves as the Compliance Advisor for iKeepSafe.

Previously, Linnette served as Vice President, Standards & Practices for Nickelodeon, and as a compliance executive with CBS.

DLG: You have expert knowledge in an area that seems very daunting and complex—government regulations. Can you please highlight the most important thing that designers and developers in the United States need to keep in mind when creating sites and apps for kids?

LA: I'd say the most important thing is, if you're going to collect data of any kind from a child, you need to talk to someone who understands the law. And do it before you start building. There is so much stuff that's now considered "personal information" (PI) under the law, and if you can be aware of that while you're putting wireframes and designs together, it's so much easier than if you try to add it at the end. If your site is already built, it's really challenging to retrofit it to work within the privacy requirements. At the beginning of a project, if you know you're going to collect data of any kind from kids, you need to account for how that's going to happen. If you build without safeguards, you then have to go back and fix it after a lot of the tech decisions have been made. I see it all the time where developers have to go back and spend time, money, and resources to redesign, and end up with a product that's not in keeping with their initial goal and that they're not happy with. When I consult after a design has been coded, many times a company isn't able to make the changes, so sometimes I have to come up with solutions that water down the design and implementation.

Talk to a compliance person about your idea before you start going down a path of design and development.

DLG: I know that the Children's Online Privacy Protection Act (COPPA) has gone through some recent revisions. Can you discuss these revisions and what they mean for people who design for kids?

LA: The proposed COPPA revisions have been accepted and have gone into effect as of July 1, 2013. All kids' sites need to be compliant. One of the most important aspects of the law that has changed is that the definition of PI has been amended. Instead of just textual data like name, address, and phone number, it now includes geolocation, as well as photos, videos, and audio files that contain the child's image or voice. If you're collecting user-generated content in the form of photos, videos, or audio, you now have to get parental consent. We're waiting to hear what the rules will be about the media that kids have already uploaded prior to these changes taking effect. We are not sure if this will be grandfathered in or if sites will have to go back and get parental consent for existing assets.

Another big change is that a user's persistent identifier (UDID or IP address) is considered to be personal info, except when used for analytics purposes. When these identifiers are used to track a child user over time for behavioral targeting, you need to get parental consent.

There have been lots of other changes, too. Plug-ins and ad networks must follow these rules if their content or functionality appears or can be accessed by kids' sites. Everyone needs to take a look to make sure they're in compliance.

It's important to be aware of how technology changes may affect data collection, too. It's hard to anticipate what new technology will be, but there will surely be additional data-collection opportunities. For people working on future platforms and new tech, I tell them to look at the rules that exist and apply all those rules to the new platform, so it will be more likely that they will be in compliance.

DLG: You mentioned ad networks. What implications do these updated COPPA regulations have on advertising to kids online?

LA: Kids don't have the cognitive capacity to understand the ramifications of advertising on online privacy. Take everything you know about compliance and apply it to whatever platform comes next. See what the requirements are now and make sure conceptually that you're meeting those rules. Kids need special protection, and businesses need to take responsibility for their audience. We're almost protecting them from ourselves.

This is a business—you have the trust of kids and parents. Don't violate that.

DLG: What responsibility do site and app owners have toward addressing the issue of cyberbullying? What are some ways that designers and developers can anticipate and prevent this in online social environments?

LA: If you're designing a product for kids and put social features in there, you need to be aware of cyberbullying and take some steps. There are three things you should do:

1. Offer education/FAQs/rules about what is and isn't acceptable behavior on your site, and then enforce those rules.

2. Build in safeguards. You need to take responsibility for how kids speak to one another by using tools like filters, dictionaries, and canned chat. Build in a lot of reporting mechanisms so kids can push a report button if someone is making them uncomfortable.

3. Watch and moderate. Kids can't be alone on a site without moderation. You can have all conversations go through moderation before they appear on the site, or you can always have a moderator on the site. And you need to act, interrupt, and address issues when they arise. This is especially important when new sites launch. You really don't know how kids are going to use your site. For example, if your differentiating factor is social gaming, you may have kids who work your system to build in competitions and trash-talk each other. You have to anticipate that kids are going to use your site in a completely different way than you envision. You have to mold the community you've created into what you want it to be, because kids won't do it themselves. You have to teach and enforce the rules.

It's important to note that we typically don't put these safeguards in place for adult audiences, so kids who lie about their ages and join FB and other sites that are not designed for kids aren't going to necessarily have a safe experience. We need to start education about online safety early and often, for kids as young as 3 or 4.

DLG: What are the key characteristics of a site or app that's "doing it right?"

LA: I'd say that appropriate levels of parental involvement and including lots of ways to report and connect with those running the site show concern and that a company has taken steps to address privacy and cyberbullying concerns.

What's especially important for designers and developers is, if there are problems on your site, address the situation and adjust accordingly, especially right after sites launch, because no matter what safeguards you put in place, kids will find a way around them. They'll push boundaries, take risks, and question the rules of conduct.

DLG: Can you talk a little bit about parental opt-in? Why is this so important? Do you think parental consent is enough to protect children's privacy online, or is it more of a minimum COPPA requirement?

LA: Parental opt-in is required any time you collect personal info from kids younger than 13. The law sets out ways that we can verify parental consent—a parent's credit card or social security number, or a form for parents to sign and fax back—these are all methods the government has designated as acceptable.

DLG: What about parental opt-in via email? Is that no longer enough?

LA: Parental email opt-in is allowable when you're collecting data for internal site purposes. But if you're sharing or transferring data, you need the extra verifiable parental opt-in.

DLG: What are the ramifications of not being COPPA compliant for sites and apps?

LA: They're pretty significant. The FTC will negotiate a settlement— usually, a monetary fine that can be as high as $3 million or as low as $50 thousand—based on the nature of the infraction and the financial situation of the company.

The FTC will also make you delete the data you've collected going back to when the act was created. So it's not just a matter of waiting until you get caught and deleting the data from that point on, you may have to fundamentally rethink the way your site works.

You'll also have to post a link from your site to onguard.online.gov. This is a consumer education site about online privacy. If you are found to be in violation of the regulations, you have to post a link to their site for five years.

You will also need to hire someone to train your staff on these issues and do compliance audits for up to 20 years. This could be a business-ending proposition. That's why it's so critical for developers and designers to talk to someone before building. Plus, these settlements are public—every parent and media outlet can find out about your violations—which means you lose credibility and trust across the board. And it's incredibly challenging to rebuild your community and regain that trust.

I haven't seen anyone deliberately break the law. It can just come down to lack of awareness, lack of proper training, and lack of auditing over time. Make sure that every time you do a redesign or add new functionality, you talk to someone about those changes. It will save you a fortune in the long run. ■

CHAPTER 7

Kids 8-10: The "Cool" Factor

Hudson, Age 8

It doesn't stop being magic just because you know how it works.

—Terry Pratchett

When kids reach age 8 or so, you start seeing a big shift in terms of cognition, confidence, and independence. They're not little kids anymore, dependent on parents and teachers; in fact, in certain areas, they are more sophisticated than the adults in their lives. They're starting to understand, accurately, the ramifications of their actions, and they realize that the world doesn't end when they don't play by the rules. This feeling is extremely liberating for the pre-'tweens. You'll see a resurgence in insecurity in the 10–12-year-olds, but the 8–10s are ready to take over the world. Look out.

Who Are They?

Children in the 8–10 range are pretty complex. They like being seen as the authorities on their favorite topics; they enjoy the "shock factor" that comes with really crazy, gross, or annoying things; and they are much less concerned about what others think of them than the 6–8s were. Table 7.1 highlights some of the 8–10 characteristics.

Getting Away with It

All this added confidence and knowledge can lead to a sense of invincibility among 8–10s. They're not particularly afraid of anything online, since it's an area they play in all the time and are inherently comfortable with. Couple this with an increased focus on identity awareness, and you've got a potentially dangerous situation on your hands. Kids as young as age 8 are accessing social media sites and apps and are being "friended" by folks they don't know. As designers, for both kids and adults, we have increased responsibility to look out for our young users. This may be the most important aspect of designing for 8–10s.

Now let's take a look at each of the characteristics in Table 7.1 and see what they mean when designing for 8–10-year-olds.

TABLE 7.1 CONSIDERATIONS FOR 8–10-YEAR-OLDS

8–10-year-olds...	This means that...	You'll want to...
Like to be the experts.	They don't read instructions; they just jump in and start doing.	Use post-failure messaging to teach instead of up-front directions.
Can take into account multiple aspects of a problem in order to solve it.	They like more complicated, challenging interfaces that require them to think.	Keep the level of complexity relatively high, but not impossible to figure out.
Can tell the difference between ads and actual content.	They're starting to dislike and distrust ads. Ads that are too numerous/too big can cause them to abandon an experience.	Create a real visual separation between ads and content.
Are starting to realize that adults don't have all the answers.	They feel more empowered to push back on rules, ideas, and directions.	Invite them to be silly. Provide opportunities for nuances instead of black-and-white rules.
Are confident enough with their interpersonal skills to be less frightened of strangers online.	They're more open to chatting online with people they know and those they don't.	Be very careful about how you introduce social elements. Even if they seem harmless, kids will find a way to get around them.
Have figured out that if they fib about themselves online, chances are no one will know.	They fib about their identity online, usually about age but sometimes about other stuff, too, just for the thrill of doing something illicit.	Put less emphasis on identity and more on self-expression and accomplishment. If you need age-gating, use parental opt-in to get demographic info.

Provide Instructions After Failure

"Failure" is probably not the right word to use here, but it's how kids will see their initial attempts to master an interface. Unlike our 6–8s, our 8–10s don't look for instructions before beginning, so they might not be completely successful the first time they use your design. While a 6-year-old probably won't try something without adequate direction, a 9-year-old will size up the interface, determine if it's worth his time, and jump right in. This presents a huge opportunity for teaching—after the kid fails the first time.

Using confirmation and error messages to provide incremental instruction is very powerful for this age group. And most kids' sites aren't doing this. Since children aren't reading directions before starting, why not use follow-up messages to teach?

I did a research study several years ago for Pepperidge Farm's *Goldfish Fun* site. The site does a great job of providing up-front instructions, but it misses a teaching opportunity with its follow-up messaging. The 9-year-olds I worked with opened the games and immediately started playing, ignoring the directions. When I asked about the directions, most of the answers included something like "Oh, this looks easy. I'll just start playing," or "I'm really good at these kinds of games." When the kids didn't perform as well as they'd liked on the games, some of them got discouraged and looked for help, while others gave up and moved on to different games altogether.

Eventually, kids gravitated to *Goldfish Fun's Catapult Chaos*—a physics game that lets players control the angle and velocity of a virtual marble launched from a spoon to knock down a bunch of items (see Figure 7.1). Kids have to try and knock down as many of the items as they can.

FIGURE 7.1
Kids ignored the contextual help on *Catapult Chaos* and clicked the "Skip Tutorial Mode" button to start playing.

Catapult Chaos followed all the rules for designing for kids. Instead of a lengthy instruction screen, it presented contextual tips for mastering the game. It demonstrated how to play through animation. But the kids ignored all of this. They just wanted to play.

During the research sessions, one little boy played this game almost the entire time. In fact, the only way I was able to tear him away from the computer was to show him the American Express gift card I had for him to thank him for his participation. He kept tweaking the position of his spoon and the power of his marble launch repeatedly to see if he could achieve the Total Takedown Bonus, awarded when the player knocked down everything at once. His tweaks were mostly random, though, and his frustration increased whenever his score decreased. He clicked on the "Help" link, but the instructions there were too general to provide any real assistance (see Figure 7.2).

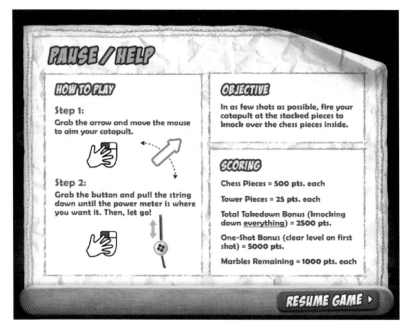

FIGURE 7.2

Catapult Chaos's instructions are too general to provide help on how to improve your score.

No messages appeared during game play, and he didn't see any type of confirmation except for a basic "nice job!" after he finished the level. He would have been able to increase both his knowledge and his score if messages were displayed periodically during the round, saying: "Try increasing your power meter this time!" or "What would happen if you tilted your spoon a little further down?" The goal here is not to provide a cheat or to minimize the exploratory aspects of the experience, but rather to set kids up for success in a meaningful way.

> **NOTE** FOLLOWING UP
>
> Using follow-up messaging as a teaching tool works for adult audiences, too. Think about the last time you filled out a form online. Did you read instructions before beginning, or did you just start entering your information? If you missed a field or entered incomplete data, did you get a general "Oops, try again" message, or did you get specific instructions on what you did wrong and how to fix it? Which did you prefer?

A team I worked with at Comcast designed an interface allowing customers with subscriptions to watch programs online. The first iteration of this system was really complicated, due to technical limitations and legal complications. Customers had to download and install two different pieces of software and log in three times. The team designed a really helpful set of instructions, but during usability testing learned that no one was reading it; rather, customers were waiting for context-based feedback to help them correct their mistakes. The team revised its approach and created a series of highly personalized "error" messages that essentially coached customers through the process. People were still frustrated, but the frustration was markedly less when the messages provided explicit information on how to recover and proceed.

Up the Complexity

Last year, I led the "Bring your kids to work day" activities at Comcast. I got to "teach" twenty-five 8–10-year-olds and their parents how to design apps. For the first part of the session, I interviewed the kids about their favorite apps. Most of these apps were games, and the games were of surprisingly high complexity, like *Jelly Car, Doodle Jump, Plants vs. Zombies, Angry Birds,* and *Minecraft.* The kids cited very few educational apps or apps that were designed specifically for kids. And when it came time for them to sketch out their ideas for new apps, the level of complexity they wanted to include was impressive. One 9-year-old (whose dad, it must be noted, is a brilliant software engineer) sketched an idea for a game that was a combination of *Angry Birds* and *Plants vs. Zombies*. It was basically impossible to play, given his explanation, and the kids were more excited about this than any of the other ideas presented.

This doesn't mean that, as designers, we should create games and apps that exist only to be difficult. Rather, for our 8–10s, we should think about activities that require dexterity, skill, accomplishment, and the ability to improve over time. If the value proposition's high enough, kids will be incredibly loyal players, at least until the next cool challenge comes along.

Let's take a look at *Pocket Frogs*, an app that lets players discover, breed, collect, and trade frogs with other players.

Pocket Frogs is pretty complicated. You collect frogs, feed and care for them, and then breed them to create even rarer species. There are all kinds of rules around which frogs can be bred with other frogs (see Figure 7.3).

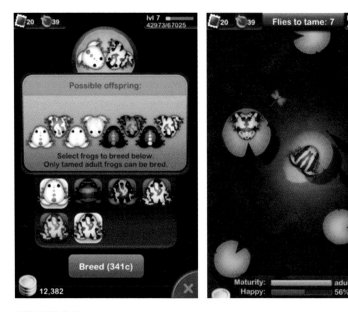

FIGURE 7.3

Pocket Frogs' complex set of breeding rules appeals to 8–10-year-olds.

The great thing about *Pocket Frogs* is that the interface itself is pretty intuitive, but the rules are quite complex. There's a whole currency system—including money, potions, and stamps—that users must figure out in order to buy stuff to keep their frogs happy. Players also have to learn which frogs are comparable in worth to other frogs in order to make reasonable trades. It's a game that can take awhile to master, but provides the opportunity for immediate and ongoing reward. Some 8–10-year-olds like this. They're not necessarily looking for a game or app that they can master right away. Younger kids love repetition and prefer to excel immediately at something that they can accomplish over and over again. When kids turn age 8 or so, they like games that provide more of a complex "journey," where they can continue to learn, grow, and discover over time.

Ads Aren't Content

Until kids reach age 5 or so, they're unable to tell the difference between commercials and regular TV programming. This is a real problem for parents and educators, because it's difficult to raise media-literate kids if they're constantly targeted by advertisers without understanding why and what it's all about. In 1992, the Children's Television Act imposed rules around advertising for kids, mandating that among other things, commercials for licensed character toys should not be shown during the programs featuring the characters—so, GI Joe toy commercials can't be shown during GI Joe cartoons. The rules have since become more stringent, and some channels featuring programming for very young children don't permit commercials targeting kids to be shown at all during these shows.

Fortunately, guidelines around TV and online advertising for kids continue to evolve. CARU, the Children's Advertising Review Unit, a U.S. organization with members across government, advertising, programming, and the private sector, publishes the *Self-Regulatory Guidelines for Children's Advertising* with information on complying with various government advertising and privacy rules. They also route consumer complaints to the proper government agencies.

Despite all these efforts, some unscrupulous advertisers/programmers still manage to get ads through. The good news, however, is that the 8–10s are pretty savvy when it comes to advertising. In fact, they'll react negatively when they see an ad unit crop up in a content area. Good news, except if you rely on ads to keep your site or app afloat.

The answer? Well, it's complicated. The best thing to do is to acknowledge the existence of ads within your experience and call them out clearly so that kids can ignore or process them as they see fit. Advertisers will want to be in compliance, so they'll most likely agree to the visual treatment you place around their ad units.

The Campbell's Soup Company's kid sites do a good job calling out advertising. They use an indicator, called "Ad Nooze," to identify the components of the site that are trying to sell instead of entertain (see Figure 7.4).

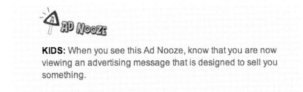

KIDS: When you see this Ad Nooze, know that you are now viewing an advertising message that is designed to sell you something.

FIGURE 7.4
On the *Goldfish Fun* site, an "Ad Nooze" indicator tells kids that they're looking at an ad.

Kids using the *Goldfish Fun* site understand that whenever they see the "Ad Nooze" indicator, they should put their savvy consumer hats on. Nickelodeon also pops up an indicator for ads, but theirs is much more subtle (see Figure 7.5)

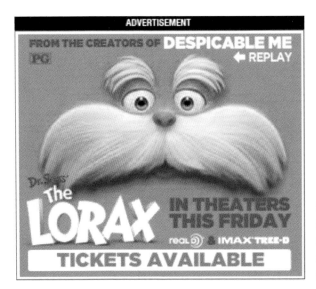

FIGURE 7.5
Nick.com's advertise-ment indicator is very small and blends into the background.

Nick.com is following CARU guidelines, but to the minimum. The word "ADVERTISEMENT" is pretty small, and a bit hard to read. Kids will figure out that this is an ad, but will be more likely to get annoyed that it's interrupting their content experience. It's best to clearly identify the ads within your interface, to meet user needs and be in compliance with government regulations.

"Poopyhead" Is a Perfectly Acceptable User Name

Kids learn, at around age 8, that adults don't always have all the answers and can sometimes be—shockingly—wrong. Instead of tacitly acknowledging this and moving on, kids tend to exploit this by pushing back. They taunt the adults in their lives with curse words they learned in the playground, they scare younger siblings with dead bugs, and they break the rules they think are dumb. While it can be hard for parents to deal with these behaviors, as designers, we have a responsibility to encourage them and let these kids rule, at least within our environments. By permitting kids to break the rules within the experiences we design, we're validating their intelligence and sophistication in the safe confines of a digital space.

Of course, you don't want the interface you design to be a free-for-all. You want all your users to feel comfortable. As a result, you'll want to curb the particularly outrageous behaviors while encouraging the silly, harmless ones.

A good way to do this is to give kids creative license when developing their online personas. If you let kids pick ridiculous user names (as long as these don't include obscenities or personally identifiable information), they'll feel as though they've trumped the system and pulled one over on the adults who are behind the experience. And they'll feel a secret thrill every time they log in with the name "poopyhead."

ROBLOX is a fantastic site where kids can create their own virtual worlds for other players to explore. They can build and program items within the world to have specific behaviors, to match their grandiose imaginations. In short, they can create a world in which anything is possible. And, while the name "poopyhead" is already taken, *ROBLOX* is quick to provide creative alternatives (see Figure 7.6).

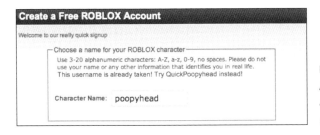

FIGURE 7.6
ROBLOX lets kids be creative when picking user names.

Another great way to let kids be the authority is to support unconventional behaviors within your experience. While the 6–8s get really uncomfortable when rules are broken, they also love it. Why can't the crazy zombie pop out of the tree trunk and scare the next-door neighbor? Or why can't the cat sprout wings and land on the teacher's head?

ROBLOX, although its interface is confusing, lets kids pretty much create and build any type of environment they want, with their own rules around behaviors, activities, and physics (see Figures 7.7 and 7.8). It is based on the concept of Constructionism, which maintains that kids learn concepts like logic, language, and math as they build things on their own.

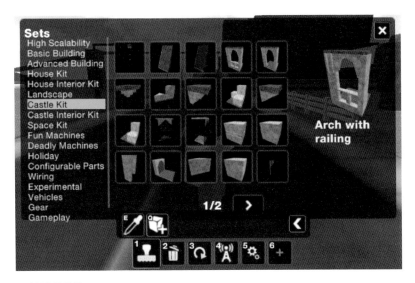

FIGURE 7.7
Kids can build their own *ROBLOX* worlds.

FIGURE 7.8
Kids can add and delete items from their *ROBLOX* worlds.

NOTE THE THEORY BEHIND IT

The theory of constructionism was developed by Dr. Seymour Papert, a professor and mathematician at MIT. Dr. Papert is considered one of the top authorities on technology and learning. In his book, *Mindstorms: Children, Computers, and Powerful Ideas*, Dr. Papert describes how kids learn complex concepts in mathematics, logic, and language by creating their own computer programs. It's definitely worth a read for anyone interested in educational technology.[1]

Despite its overall awesomeness, *ROBLOX* is pretty hard to use across the board. It's got a steep learning curve, despite the common icons and symbols it uses to communicate functionality. A typical 9-year-old will have a difficult time figuring out how to get started building stuff. I got confused simply trying to move items around on the screen, and somehow invoked the situation in Figure 7.9.

I do like how the system provides feedback on the user's actions after she performs them. Although kids like to jump in, do stuff, and learn how to improve after failing, I'm not sure a 9-year-old would be able to understand what to do here. It would be great if the error

---

1 Seymour Papert, *Mindstorms: Children, Computers, and Powerful Ideas* (Brighton: Harvester Press, 1980).

messages in the *ROBLOX* code contained some teaching information, like "This means you need to close the builder menu before continuing." Overall, though, the idea and spirit behind *ROBLOX* is exciting and inspiring. Letting kids build and explore their own environments supports how the 8–10s behave and allows them to be experts within their own domain.

FIGURE 7.9
I have no idea what this screen is telling me.

Of course, you may not have the ability, budget, or license to design a completely open system where kids can control the behavior of their characters or elements. However, you can incorporate some of these ideas on a smaller scale. Let them be silly, give them chances to run the show even in small bursts—for example, user names, avatars, and so on—and celebrate their unconventional behaviors and ideas.

A Matter of Trust

While the 6–8s are scared of people they don't know, the 8–10s tend to be more gregarious and social, especially online. Since the Internet is a domain they know, better, possibly, than the adults in their lives, they're pretty confident in their abilities to use it. This confidence includes communicating with people online. How can a device as trusted and well known as a computer or tablet hurt them in any way, especially given their expertise in the space? As a designer, you need to be aware of this, not just when designing kid sites, but when designing any site with a social component.

I did some research using the Club Penguin site about a year ago. One 8-year-old boy, who was uncharacteristically reluctant to communicate with other players, even using the canned chat mechanism, told me a story about how his sister, who was 10 at the time, gave the family phone number to a man she met online. The man called, their dad answered the phone, got the guy's number and gave it to his brother who happened to be an FBI agent. Uncle FBI Agent came over the next day and scared the crap out of these kids about giving personal information out online. "If you talk to people online, they'll find out where you live and come to your house and steal your stuff," the kid told me.

Most of your users probably won't have FBI agents in their family, but it's still your responsibility (and legal obligation) to protect them online.

So how do you engage these outgoing, social, technologically confident kids in your designs? Carefully. Age-gating and parental consent aren't enough, because, as you'll see in a bit, these kids fib (aka outright lie). If you're designing a site for kids, "social" should only be a component, an enhancement to your site's main purpose. Kids will emphasize the social piece if they find the rest of the experience boring or "too babyish." To them, being social online means being mature and grown-up. Those are the main value propositions of any social component for kids. So, if you make your experience itself feel "grown-up," the social component will be less of an allure. To do this, you'll want to make sure that your design isn't patronizing or condescending, and you should use simple, plain language that doesn't try too hard to sound cool.

Everloop is a site designed to give kids between 8 and 13 the "social network experience" within a safe, monitored, parentally controlled environment (see Figure 7.10). The concepts behind it are really strong. Kids can join various "loops" to communicate with like-minded people, and parents can control the level of engagement their kids can have, restricting IM usage and requesting notifications when their kids make new friends.

This is all very good. However, what the site's design communicates is, "Hey kids, you're too immature to use 'real' sites like *Facebook*, so here's this lame, dumbed-down version with music and videos, because that's what you kids like."

FIGURE 7.10
Everloop's goals are noble, but its design talks down to kids.

This site was clearly designed by well-meaning adults who believe they know what kids like and want. Using the phrase "Just for Us," while communicating the value proposition of the site, will deter kids from engaging, since it's so obviously targeting kids. Kids will gravitate toward the chat and networking functionality here since the self-referential games, goobs (pranks you can play on your friends), and videos are presented in a rather condescending way. Using a color scheme that's similar to Facebook, and including functionality that's similar to Facebook, merely reinforces the fact that this, in fact, is *not* Facebook, but rather a "lite" version. This is the kind of site that parents love and kids hate.

If the design focused more on what it offers instead of pushing the "for kids" angle, kids would be more excited to participate in the loops and features and less interested in the chatting and messaging components. And thus, they'd be *less* likely to chat with people they didn't know, simply for the sake of doing so, and focus more on the common interests and elements that brought them together.

It's OK to Lie if Nobody Gets Hurt

I remember the first time I saw a kid fib in a user-research session. Alyssa was 9, and we were looking at sites that required registration in order to play games. When filling out the registration form, Alyssa said she was 11, and that she lived in New Jersey, not Pennsylvania. These little fibs were minor, and would have no impact on the site Alyssa was trying to access. I asked her why she had lied. "Well," she said, "It's okay to lie if nobody gets hurt." When I probed further, Alyssa explained that she really didn't know why she had lied about her age and state, but she just "felt like it."

This happens a lot. The idea of lying about who you are online and having *nothing bad happen* because of it is extremely powerful to these kids, who, for the most part, are honest and well meaning in their real-world interactions. There's a certain thrill associated with saying you're 11 when you're really 9. This situation presents interesting implications for designers, even when designing experiences meant for adult audiences, because ultimately, you never really know who your users are.

Kids will mostly lie about who they are, not about what grade they're in or what their interests are. They also tend to stay true to their gender, since that is such a key component of their identity. But things like age, location, and physical appearance are completely up for grabs.

This isn't necessarily a bad thing. Experimenting with these things in the context of the Internet lets kids explore concepts of identity in a relatively safe environment. Where they run into trouble is on sites like Facebook, where kids have to be at least 13 in order to participate. In this case, a little white lie can lead to unwanted interactions. There are rules and regulations for these types of environments, but it's hard for site administrators to weed out everyone who may or may not be lying about their age, as this could be almost anyone. And since most sites' Terms and Conditions and EULAs (end-user license agreements) are walls of text, few people, let alone kids, read them all the way through.

The best way to get around this is to emphasize the more interesting aspects of identity and downplay characteristics like age and location. Collecting demographic information is important when deciding what content to show to specific users, or for marketing purposes, but if you place less importance on this and more on the other components of a child's identity, you'll reduce the likelihood of harmless fibbing.

The *Candystand* site, geared toward kids ages 8 and up, has a pretty standard registration process (see Figure 7.11.)

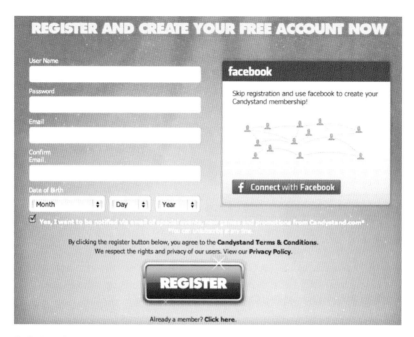

FIGURE 7.11

Kids will probably lie about their age on the *Candystand* registration page.

Chances are, if kids are going to lie, they'll put in an incorrect birthday here. The form is simple enough, but asks for just enough information to be annoying. Kids don't understand why they have to register to use sites anyway, and if they feel like they're being judged because of their age, or that they might not be able to use all site features if they're too young, they'll make up a birth date.

A better approach here would be to put the emphasis on the user name, since that's where kids can be most creative. They can create a password and then do something fun, like pick their Zodiac sign, or click an image of what the weather's like on their birthday. They can then select the year. Letting them be creative in other areas of the registration process will make them less likely to want to be creative in selecting their birth year or location. If you need a parent's email address, make a space for them to enter it, but create some basic features of the site that they can use without parental consent. When they try to access an area that requires a parent's approval, you can then prompt them for the email address. This breaks up the process while still setting them up for success. Which, ultimately, is your primary goal as experience designers.

Oh, and that Facebook module on the right? As we discussed earlier, *Facebook's* Terms & Conditions mandate a minimum age of 13 in order to use their services. When you're designing for kids, and your experience requires registration, don't encourage them to sign in with a Facebook account. It doesn't matter that some of them already have Facebook accounts. You're encouraging them to violate the T&Cs, and that's probably not a great idea. Build your own registration process. If kids are excited enough about what your site will let them do, they'll register. And if you design wisely, they'll even use real data.

PARENTS ARE USERS, TOO

If you're a parent of a child between the ages of 8 and 10, chances are you've seen a parental opt-in email. These messages alert parents to the fact that their children have signed up to use a site with a community component, where they can save or store personal data, artwork, or photos, or where they may be able to interact with others. These messages also give parents basic information about the site's goals, mission, and benefits, as well as how they can access the site and see what their child has been up to.

Most of these emails have long disclaimers, privacy policies, terms and conditions, as well as detailed information about how to monitor their child's behavior. I haven't seen many instances of well-designed parental opt-in emails, but the folks at *DIY* do a great job with theirs (see Figure 7.12). Written in plain language, this opt-in message tells a story—what the site is, how it works, and what role their child plays in the overall experience.

The basic grid, big and clear buttons, and easy-to-read text ensure that parents will actually take a few minutes to understand how it might benefit their child to use *DIY*. If the email were more cluttered or filled with more legalese, parents might be less likely to give their consent for their children to participate. But with this email, *DIY* shows it has nothing to hide. While COPPA only requires that a company send an email, if you, as a designer, pay attention to the design and messaging, it will help busy parents cut through the clutter and understand what their kids are doing online.

Your kid joined DIY!

DIY is a community where young makers do challenges and earn Skills. Please verify that it's OK for them to join.

 ✓ Activate

Verification link:
https://parents.diy.org/verify/fcae54b7-24cb-4a57-941b-ce0cc86f8f41

Important Details

Avatar
Your kid chose a raccoon.

Nickname
They have a DIY nickname, too.

Magnolia Guardian

DIY Member

Password
Their account is protected with a password. You can change it anytime in your Parent Dashboard.

Portfolio
Once you verify, their portfolio will be public at diy.org/magnoliaguardian

iOS App
Download our app! This is the easiest way for your kid to capture what they make and and share.

Skills
Also, check out all the Skills they can earn. Help your kid do any three Skill challenges and they'll earn the patch!

Want to receive less email?
Adjust your notification settings.

Forget your password?
We'll help you reset it.

Need help?
Email Us!

Receive important updates

FIGURE 7.12
DIY's parental consent email helps parents understand the site's purpose.

On Gender, Complexity, and Discovery

There's been lots of controversy lately on toys, games, and interfaces targeting girls. While I believe it's lazy and presumptuous for toy companies to slap pink on something, dumb it down a little, and call it "For Girls," there are marked differences in how girls and boys prefer to play. Girls tend to prefer games requiring exploration, discovery, and collaboration while boys prefer competition, action, and advancement. Also, boys like to use their advanced spatial skills during play while girls prefer to use complex reasoning.

To get past this, you should design as you would for adults, by understanding your target users' needs, behaviors, and attitudes. Design for how kids play, rather than who they are. For example, if you want to create an experience that appeals to girls, develop complex problems for them to solve based on relationships and connections. *Webkinz* does this well, as does *Pocket Frogs*— kids have to control multiple variables to keep their pets happy and safe, which is the ultimate value proposition (see Figure 7.13).

FIGURE 7.13
Webkinz's emphasis on connection, care, and discovery appeals to the way that girls play.

If you want to create experiences targeting boys, include more opportunities for traditional game-play focusing on immediate gratification, timed competitions, races, and anything "physical" (knocking stuff down, blowing stuff up, and so on). *Tank Hero* (best for kids 9 and up due to some mild violence) definitely accomplishes this (see Figure 7.14).

FIGURE 7.14

Tank Hero focuses on both strategy and physical ability, which boys enjoy.

Chances are, if you're designing an experience for kids, you're looking to meet the needs of both genders. You'll want to examine the overall project and user goals and determine which experience would best accomplish them. If your goals are broad, like "learn multiplication," you'll have an easier time crafting experiences involving both action and discovery. If your goals are more specific, like "create complex structures using all these different parts and share them with others," you'll want to think about the behaviors these goals support and design accordingly.

Like design itself, gender differences aren't black and white. Girls enjoy shoot-'em-up games as much as boys like exploration. The key is to make sure that your interface supports differences in play style, skills, and preferred behaviors of your users.

Chapter Checklist

As you've seen, designing for 8–10-year-olds is a completely different endeavor than designing for younger—and, as we'll see in a moment, older— kids. When creating sites and apps for these children, make sure that you address the following information.

Does your design cover the following areas?

☐ Provide contextual help after failure?

☐ Feature complex, but not impossible, challenges?

☐ Separate ads from actual site or app content?

☐ Invite silliness and/or irreverence?

☐ Include limitations on social interactions?

☐ Emphasize self-expression and accomplishment?

Now let's take a look at the oldest age group, the 10–12-year-olds. As you'll see, these guys are very complex and sophisticated, with highly developed cognitive skills, but they still need some special treatment when it comes to design.

Favorite App: *Fluff Rescue*

Iris is a very sophisticated 9-year-old. She loves to read, draw, hang out with her friends, peruse the *New York Times* Health section, and play games on her family's iPad; preferably, games that involve a lot of complex problem solving. "I like games that keep on going and that don't just end," she said.

Iris's current favorite is a game called *Fluff Rescue* (see Figures 7.15 and 7.16). "I like it because it feels like you're helping," she said. "You're giving a pet with no home a home, and you get to raise them. You feel satisfied because it means you're helping."

FIGURE 7.15

Fluff Rescue lets kids adopt, build homes, and care for pets.

sidebar continues on next page

The premise? "You get to adopt animals and keep them in your backyard or sell them. Animals wander around, and when you see one you want to adopt, you click on it to buy it. If you have enough money, it goes into the station for what its condition is to get healed." The app has a complex currency system that Iris has figured out: "Money is worth a lot more in *Fluff Rescue* than it is in a game like *Dragonvale* because things cost less. So 5,000 coins probably equals 100,000 coins in *Dragonvale*. It's simple. You don't get as much money in *Fluff Rescue*."

Helping animals, solving problems, making money, and discovering story lines are all part of what makes the game exciting for Iris. "You have to learn to understand stuff and make choices. You have to decide whether to buy something that costs more money if you think you're going to get more money."

FIGURE 7.16
Kids have to make sure their pets are fed and happy in order to earn currency in *Fluff Rescue*.

Iris approaches games and apps the way many 8–10-year-old girls do—she finds one she loves and plays it whenever she gets the chance. She immerses herself in the experience over time and finds reward in the small achievements of caring for a pet and finding it a home. And *Fluff Rescue* lends itself perfectly to the schedule of a kid busy with school, family, extra-curricular activities, drawing, and reading. "When I find an app I like, I play it a lot. I collect money every day. When I get a new game, it becomes part of tradition. It's like brushing my teeth or washing my hands."

In addition to apps, Iris likes dorkdiaries.com because it lets her delve deeper into the *Dork Diaries* book series, learn more about the characters, read the blog, and get updates. "*Dork Diaries* is for older kids, because the books are longer, and they have complicated problems."

The themes that Iris looks for in the apps she downloads are narrative, continuity, problem-solving, balancing complex needs, and earning/exchanging currency. Some of this speaks to gender, as girls tend to prefer the detailed and complex to the quick and exciting, but it also reflects cognitive maturity and the need for greater challenges.

Kids 10–12: Growing Up

Zachary, Age 10

> Reality has always been too small for the human imagination. We're always trying to transcend.
>
> —Brenda Laurel

Kids 10–12 are challenging for parents and designers alike when it comes to technology. These guys are not little kids anymore, and they don't want to be treated that way. They tend to spend more time with apps like *Snapchat* and *Instagram* than they do on media geared toward kids. They use popular apps and games, but are starting to use technology more as a tool for information and communication than for entertainment. It's becoming harder for parents to keep track of what their kids are doing digitally, since most of what kids do is on a smartphone or a mobile device. Parental controls, while effective, can undermine the trust that a parent has placed in a child, and this further complicates what's already becoming a complicated relationship. Welcome to adolescence.

Who Are They?

As kids get older, it's harder to pin down exactly who they are and what they need. Similar to designing for adults, doing research on the specific activities you're designing for kids becomes more important to understand their expectations. Table 8.1 features some general guidelines to start with.

Take The Guesswork Out

Kids 10–12 are becoming masters of abstract thought. They're able to interpret complex scenarios and imagine all the possible outcomes of their actions and decisions. This new ability to see things from other perspectives means that they sometimes agonize over what to do. Designing for these guys can be challenging, because while you want to build in flexibility for choice, you also don't want to incapacitate your users so they're unable to make a decision.

So, how do you get around this? How do you create designs that are engaging and complex without creating discomfort and indecision? The answer is simple: keep it simple. Let's look at some examples.

TABLE 8.1 CONSIDERATIONS FOR 10–12-YEAR-OLDS

10–12-year-olds...	This means that...	You'll want to...
Can imagine the outcome of particular actions and decisions.	They think and deliberate before acting.	Take the guesswork out. Provide opportunity for complex decision making, but use simple design techniques.
Can think creatively.	They like to build their own scenarios and determine what the outcomes should be.	Think about the "story" your interface is telling. Is it sequential? Are there multiple pathways?
Have started using mobile devices much more than their computers.	They experience most digital interfaces on a smaller, more intimate level.	Even if you're creating a website, design for mobile screens first.
Are starting to become very aware of the things that make them "different."	They're starting to feel like misfits, as if no one understands who they are and what they're about.	Celebrate individuality. Focus less on black-and-white answers and more on situation and context.
See themselves less as "generalists" and more as "specialists."	As part of their self-identification process, they have honed in on the things that they like, the things that they're good at, and the interests that make them who they are.	Steer away from basic and general content and focus on particular areas of interest, such as art, music, science, animals, and so on.

Kingdom Rush is perfect for the 10–12s (see Figure 8.1). It involves strategy, design, fantasy, bad guys, a little bit of blood, and lots of adventure. Kids have to protect their kingdoms from goblins and orcs by strategically building towers and enhancements on the road to the castle. The design is just detailed enough to be interesting, but the interface itself is simple, allowing users to focus more on the game's objectives and less on figuring out how to do stuff. Since this game relies on strategic thinking, keeping the experience basic enables kids to consider their decisions and options instead of focusing on an overly designed, complex interface.

FIGURE 8.1

Kingdom Rush's subtle design lets kids focus on strategy.

Based on their budget and on the type of enemy approaching the kingdom, kids have to choose what type of tower to build and where. Each tower has certain properties better suited to specific types of protection. As the enemy approaches, players can see how well what they've chosen to build will perform (see Figure 8.2).

Kingdom Rush uses representational, cartoon-like graphics to teach some interesting stuff like financial management, physics, and strategy. It taps right into the complex problem-solving skills these kids have developed and lets them imagine, interpret, and understand the consequences of their decisions in an interface that requires little-to-no interpretation.

Let's contrast that with *Machinarium* (see Figure 8.3). *Machinarium* may be one of the most beautiful games ever. It's got everything—gorgeous graphics, compelling storyline, intriguing characters—but it's tough for 10–12s since the decision points are nuanced and unclear.

FIGURE 8.2
Kids use their deductive reasoning to build towers to save the kingdom from enemies.

FIGURE 8.3
Machinarium's detailed interface makes decisions difficult for 10–12s.

The goal of the game is to help an exiled robot solve puzzles and collect items so he can get back to his city and rescue his girlfriend. Users explore and uncover wonderful environments to find the clues and save the day.

For concrete thinkers, like the 6–8s, this game is perfect. They take every decision at face value and plug along, enjoying the journey. For the 10–12s, who ponder the ramifications of every decision, this game can be agonizing. There are so many things to do and so many decisions to interpret that it can quickly become overwhelming. It's interesting, because the designers of this game are clearly targeting a slightly older audience—there are veiled references to mature themes like smoking and drug use, and some of the puzzles require abstract thought—but younger kids seem to gravitate toward it. My friend's 5-year-old son loves the game and can play it for hours, but another friend's 11-year-old tried it for a few minutes and gave up.

This discrepancy occurs because games based on pure exploration are a little intimidating for the 'tweens. In fact, they reflect on every decision point, and it can paralyze them. The interface is so finely wrought that kids 10–12 become too focused on what to do next instead of simply allowing the narrative to carry them through.

Don't get me wrong, *Machinarium's* an amazing game for kids and adults. It's just a bit too open and exploratory for people who have just formed the ability to visualize multiple scenarios and implications of their actions. If you're targeting 'tweens, you'll want to sacrifice some of the exploration and focus more on promoting creativity through decision making.

Let Kids Tell Their Story

One thing *Machinarium* does really well is to unfold its narrative and storyline. Kids can experience the adventure in a way that has meaning to them. *Machinarium's* interface can cause discord as kids try to make the right choices, but if your design focuses primarily on the story (and uses the visuals to support this story), you'll make 10–12s very happy. In addition to the ability to imagine different outcomes associated with their actions, 'tweens can also think creatively. They like to craft their own scenarios and figure out different ways to negotiate an experience. While the younger users are primarily interested in the journey, the 10–12s are starting to become focused on the outcome and the destination. Your job as designers is to make this destination as interesting and desirable as possible, allowing 'tweens to use their creativity to find their way through.

Some great work is being done in this area. For example, I really like *Skrappy*, an app that lets kids curate their own media in a meaningful way by telling their own stories (see Figure 8.4.)

FIGURE 8.4

Skrappy lets kids organize their photos, videos, and music around their life stories.

Children can choose from a variety of templates and import their videos, audio, and photos into a multimedia scrapbook. The design of the interface supports this goal without overwhelming users, letting them focus on the task at hand, as well as their own creative sensibilities. The great thing about *Skrappy* is that it offers suggestions, but doesn't try to force users into particular directions based on the nature of their media (see Figure 8.5). It offers multiple pathways through the established narrative and invites users to experiment with these.

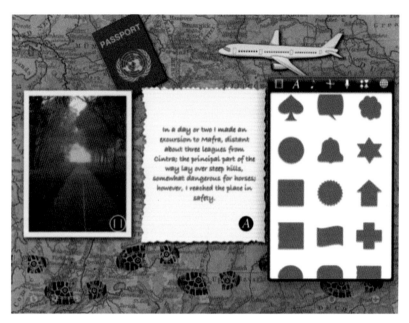

FIGURE 8.5
Kids can create their own pathways through *Skrappy's* interface.

Skrappy handles multiple decision points, creative exploration, and personal narrative very well. The options are somewhat limited as of this writing, but as the designers continue to evolve the app, I think you'll see some additional selections, allowing for even more self-expression.

Contrast that with *Photo Grid – Collage Maker*, which limits users' engagement with the app and forces them to go down set linear pathways with little opportunity for kids to express themselves (see Figure 8.6). For kids who are obsessed with *Instagram* and other self-expression and sharing tools, this app seems like a no-brainer—take your photos and make them into cool collages to send to friends and family. However, the small number of canned templates, limited ability to customize the collages, contrived and juvenile assets available to add to the collages, as well as the ads that appear at the top of the screen make this app feel very confining and linear. This app is great for adults who want to dash off a quick collection of baby pictures to the in-laws, but feels oppressively constrained for our 'tweens.

Interestingly, I had a blast with this app. I appreciated how quickly and easily I could create collages, I enjoyed the campy visuals I could add, and I liked how polished my finished product looked. But, as an adult, I value things like speed and immediate gratification while our 10–12-year-olds prefer to focus on ways to express and differentiate themselves. It's another example of how you cannot assume that your users want what you want and like what you like, especially if those users are kids.

FIGURE 8.6
Photo Grid – Collage Maker is a bit too limiting for 10–12s, but perfect for adults.

PARENTS ARE USERS, TOO

When kids enter their 'tween years, the role of parents starts becoming even more complicated. Since kids of this age are starting to break away from parental control—many start choosing to do the exact opposite of what their parents ask them to do—it's important to involve the parents and their concerns in what you architect, but in a way that doesn't interfere with the child's experience. For example, on some of the sites and apps you looked at earlier in the book, you've seen content geared toward parents, asking for their permission or just informing them about the experience and how it works.

With this age group, you'll still want to include parents, but do it from the kids' perspective. For example, instead of creating a section called "Parents," or "For Parents," you can create content directed toward kids, called "For Your Parents," or "Give This to Your Parents," so that the 'tween is in control of managing the relationship between parents and the experience. You don't want to do anything to erode the trust between your app and your audience, so allowing kids to mediate the communication or even just informing them of what you're doing goes a long way. (For example, "We're going to send an email to your parents to get their permission for you to use our app. Tell them it's coming and that it's awesome.") It will also empower more cautious parents to have the hard conversations about online privacy, predators, and purchasing.

Mobile First

Kids 10–12 use their cell phones much more frequently than they use their computers. In 2011, The Pew Internet & American Life Project[1] estimated that 78% of all teens and 'tweens have cell phones, and 23% have smartphones. That number is increasing annually, and the fastest-growing segment is the 10–12s. So what does that mean? Well, when thinking about the experiences you're designing, make sure that you focus first on how it will work on a mobile device. Think about the context in which your young users will be accessing it. Are they on the school bus? In the cafeteria at lunch? Hanging out on the couch post-homework?

The mobile-first rule doesn't just apply to apps. If you're designing a site for 10–12s, you'll want to think about how it appears on smaller screens first. Focusing on mobile will make it easier for you to identify the most important aspects of the experience, since screen real estate is more limited; it will help you cut out extraneous functionality you might have added had you been designing for a larger screen.

Let's take a look at *giantHello*, a basic social networking site for 'tweens (see Figure 8.7). The designers of this site didn't create their mobile experience first. This fact is obvious, because in order to make the links and buttons on *giantHello* remotely touchable on a smartphone, users have to enlarge the page so much that most of it is cut off.

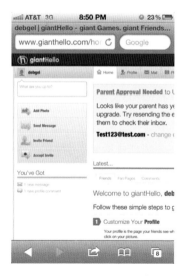

FIGURE 8.7

The *giantHello* site is cut off on a smartphone browser

---

1 http://www.pewinternet.org/Reports/2013/Teens-and-Tech.aspx

When kids are on their computers, they'll probably enjoy using this site, but since so much of their Web browsing and site usage is done on a mobile device, this site will quickly become cumbersome.

Not a lot of children's sites are "mobile first." As we see a move toward more and more sites using a responsive design framework, this will probably change, but in the current ecosystem, most sites geared toward 10–12s don't function well on mobile.

There will be certain tasks your experience requires that will most likely have to be completed on a computer or at least a tablet. Things like registration, parental consent, or anything requiring the input of large amounts of data will be better served on a device with an actual keyboard. My recommendation is to figure out the main stuff first—the pathways through the actual experience, the interactions, the tasks—and worry about the supplemental stuff last. That way, you can be sure the important aspects are mobile-friendly.

Celebrate Individuality

This need to celebrate individuality might be the most important thing to consider when designing for kids between 10 and 12. As any parent of a pre-teen will tell you, and as you might vividly recall from your 'tween years, kids in this age group are starting to come to terms with their personal differences. A perfectly "normal," well-adjusted kid may start acting out in subtle ways starting at around age 10. Even kids who don't exhibit any outward signs of rebellion are starting to feel more self-conscious, more noticeable, and more different than they used to. And the only way to address this in a digital space is to celebrate these differences.

When kids start feeling like misfits (and they all do, at some time or other), what you'll want to do is let them discover activities that have meaning for them. We already discussed the importance of allowing kids to create their own personal narratives within digital environments, but it's also important to start steering away from "right and wrong" or "black and white" and hone in instead on the gray areas in between.

This is also the age when some kids start becoming anxious about standardized tests, simply because they can see multiple outcomes of a given scenario and struggle with finding the specific right answer. The best experiences address this by self-discovery and by letting kids encounter and experience information in a way that resonates with their individual styles without, of course, making them anxious about whether the decisions they make within the experience are right or wrong.

I love *Star Walk* for kids (and adults) of all ages, but it's especially great for the 10–12s. Basically, this app lets kids hold up their iPad to the sky and see the stars and planets directly above, almost like a window into space (see Figure 8.8). The imagery and music are mysterious, almost mystical, and let users form a very personal and very real relationship with astronomy. This intimacy and this celebration of the nuances among planets and constellations resonates with kids and lets them feel as though their individuality is beautiful as well.

FIGURE 8.8
Star Walk lets kids navigate the stars in an intimate, meaningful way.

Another wonderful example of designing for individuality is *The Elements*, an app created to teach users about the Periodic Table (see Figure 8.9). Like *Star Walk,* it gives kids a very personal, very different, very connected view into all the elements in the periodic table and celebrates the unique qualities and properties of each element. Even the most basic element is breathtakingly beautiful, and coupled with tons of detailed information, makes something as mundane as Tungsten absolutely amazing.

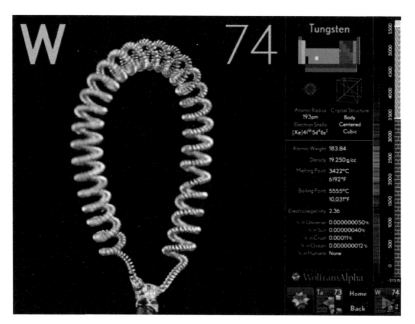

FIGURE 8.9

The Elements invites kids to explore and discover the Periodic Table.

Kids can choose to view the elements as quick overviews, with lovely photos and basic information, or they can delve deeper into longer explanations of the history and nature of each element (see Figure 8.10).

The photos, descriptions, and narratives for each element are so individualized and so finely crafted, it's obvious the creators have a great fondness for them. This approach helps kids form a personal attachment to these elements and almost associate a personality to them, which is a great way to instill the love of science and learning.

TIP DANGEROUS APPS

There's been a surge of interest among pre-teens in anonymous chat apps—like *KiK Messenger, Yik Yak, Whisper,* and *Omegle*—that let users message and share photos with strangers who live nearby. For these kids, who struggle with identity and crave attention, apps like these can create dangerous situations, frightening for parents and kids alike. If you have any type of chat mechanism available in your design, you'll want to make sure that you've got levels of content moderation and abuse reporting in place.

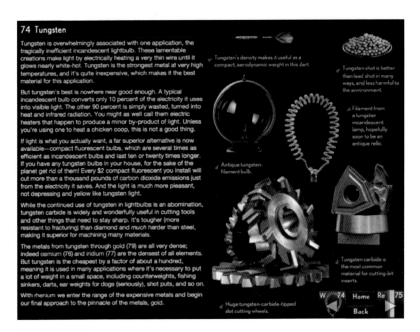

74 Tungsten

Tungsten is overwhelmingly associated with one application, the tragically inefficient incandescent lightbulb. These lamentable creations make light by electrically heating a very thin wire until it glows nearly white-hot. Tungsten is the strongest metal at very high temperatures, and it's quite inexpensive, which makes it the best material for this application.

But tungsten's best is nowhere near good enough. A typical incandescent bulb converts only 10 percent of the electricity it uses into visible light. The other 90 percent is simply wasted, turned into heat and infrared radiation. You might as well call them electric heaters that happen to produce a minor by-product of light. Unless you're using one to heat a chicken coop, this is not a good thing.

If light is what you actually want, a far superior alternative is now available—compact fluorescent bulbs, which are several times as efficient as incandescent bulbs and last ten or twenty times longer. If you have any tungsten bulbs in your house, for the sake of the planet get rid of them! Every $2 compact fluorescent you install will cut more than a thousand pounds of carbon dioxide emissions just from the electricity it saves. And the light is much more pleasant, not depressing and yellow like tungsten light.

While the continued use of tungsten in lightbulbs is an abomination, tungsten carbide is widely and wonderfully useful in cutting tools and other things that need to stay sharp. It's tougher (more resistant to fracturing) than diamond and much harder than steel, making it superior for machining many materials.

The metals from tungsten through gold (79) are all very dense; indeed osmium (76) and iridium (77) are the densest of all elements. But tungsten is the cheapest by a factor of about a hundred, meaning it is used in many applications where it's necessary to put a lot of weight in a small space, including counterweights, fishing sinkers, darts, ear weights for dogs (seriously), shot puts, and so on.

With rhenium we enter the range of the expensive metals and begin our final approach to the pinnacle of the metals, gold.

Tungsten's density makes it useful as a compact, aerodynamic weight in this dart.

Tungsten shot is better than lead shot in many ways, and less harmful to the environment.

Filament from a tungsten incandescent lamp, hopefully soon to be an antique relic.

Antique tungsten-filament bulb.

Tungsten carbide is the most common material for cutting-bit inserts.

Huge tungsten-carbide-tipped slot cutting wheels.

W 74 Home Re 75
Back

FIGURE 8.10

In *The Elements*, kids can view detailed descriptions of the elements they want to explore further.

Specialize

While *Star Walk* and *The Elements* do a great job of allowing users to celebrate their individuality and build relationships with the world around them, their appeal extends to those kids who are truly interested in these subjects. Since children ages 10–12 are starting to figure out what makes them special, and since what they like and what they do are part of what makes them special, it's important to create sites and apps for these kids that are highly focused and individualized in terms of content. For example, my cousin Kara, who is now an amazing, creative, brilliant adult, self-identified as a slam poet when she was about 12. She found something she was interested in and good at and focused her energies on developing her talent in that area, since that was how she saw herself. Kids prefer apps that allow them to do the things that make them feel special about themselves.

Along with the desire to use apps that support their individuality comes the desire to avoid apps that don't support it. For example, if an 11-year-old-boy prefers writing to geometry, it's going to be very hard to get him to download your geometry game. It's also going to be very hard to get him to download any app that's not focused on his areas of interest, regardless of how interesting those apps may be.

When setting up your absorption sessions with kids of this age group, make sure that you've identified a clear and narrow area of focus, and recruit kids with strong interest in that area. Otherwise, you will get fragmented data that will not allow you to architect an optimal experience for these kids.

Chapter Checklist

When designing for this group, think about how your design addresses the following issues.

Does your design do the following?

- ☐ Provide opportunity for complex decision making, but via a simple interface?
- ☐ Feature different narratives with multiple pathways?
- ☐ Accommodate mobile screens?
- ☐ Focus on context and situation instead of right/wrong answers?
- ☐ Address a narrow area of interest to make kids interested in this area feel special?

Favorite App: *Instagram*

Alexa is a very outgoing, social 10-year-old girl who loves to dance, take pictures, and spend time with her family and friends. Her favorite app is *Instagram*. Alexa and I talked at length about how she uses *Instagram*, what she likes about it, and how it works. She walked me through her typical *Instagram* upload process and showed me all the steps she takes to share photos. We also talked about privacy implications around sharing, rules, and unwanted followers.

"I love *Instagram*. You get to look at your friends' pictures and see different things. I like to post pictures. I think it's really cool that all your friends can look at your pictures and see what you're doing," she said. "Like, if I take a picture with my cousins, I can tell my friends that I'm at my grandmother's house at a party."

I asked her how she felt about people knowing where she was at any given time. She said, "Well, the app knows where you are, but it won't share that location with people. You just mark it as private, and it won't share it with anyone but your friends. If you're not private, then you're public and anyone can follow you."

Alexa showed me how you follow and block people on *Instagram*. She had a remarkable grasp of how to use the tool and how to make sure that no one she didn't know could follow her. "There's a box and a button. You press the button, and a big list of people comes up. If you press on a person's account, you can read all about them, how many followers they have, and you can look at their picture. There's a checkmark and an X—see?—and if you would like to follow them, you press the checkbox, and they follow. If you press the X, they can't follow you.

"My parents want to check my pictures and videos before I post them. My mom has an *Instagram* account, and she can check my and my sister's Instagrams to check the pictures too," Alexa said.

Alexa's parents are reasonable, but cautious, about how she uses the app, and have done a great job of educating her about the people she might encounter. "There are a lot of people out there who are faking things," Alexa said. "Like, there are all these Dance Mom users, but only one is the real Dance Mom. There are also lots of Justin Biebers out there with Justin Bieber as their user name and a picture of Justin Bieber, but you can't trust any of them or tell them anything about you." Alexa has developed a strategy for figuring out if a user is "real" or "fake." "You have to see the kinds of pictures they post," she said. "With the Dance Moms, it's kind of obvious. If they're the real Dance Mom, they will have pictures that you can't just get anywhere on the Internet. You can also tell by their videos and stuff."

Alexa likes to experiment with apps to figure out how they work. If she sees a button with a shape or icons she doesn't recognize, she taps on it to find out what it does. "I learned what all these buttons were by just trying them out," she said. She shows me the Explore button, which allows users to see a list of other accounts that might interest them. "There's another button that you press, and there are all these people in one row. You really don't want to look at those pictures," she says. "This just brings up a bunch of random people that nobody knows who they are or why they are there. Sometimes they are kind of naked." (There were, in fact, several images of scantily clad women.)

Themes of creation, narrative, sharing, and flow appealed to Alexa. She loves to take pictures, modify them using *Instagram* filters, and share them with her friends. Like many kids her age who are just discovering the concept of virtual communities, Alexa has uncovered elements that make her uncomfortable, but she has empowered herself to make the right decisions about whom to follow and whom to block.

Dear Dad Dad I

CHAPTER 9

Design Research

Savannah, Age 8

Play is the highest form of research.

—Albert Einstein

There are as many ways to conduct research with kids as there are types of kids. Basically, as long as you have a chance to watch kids play and hear them talk, chances are you're on the right track. If you tailor your research and testing activities to the cognitive, physical, and technical skills of the age group you're designing for, you'll have success.

Note that the research covered in this chapter is design research, and is focused on specific techniques that work especially well with kids. There are many tools, methodologies, activities, and approaches to conducting user research, but only a subset of these are addressed here. For additional information about user research, check out Mike Kuniavsky's fantastic book, *Observing the User Experience*[1] or Leah Buley's excellent book, *The User Experience Team of One*.[2]

General Guidelines

So what does it mean to conduct design research with children? In Chapter 1, "Kids and Design," we touched on this a bit, as we reviewed the Absorb and Assess stages of the design process. And while there's not a cookie-cutter approach to doing research with children, there are some activities that work better with this audience.

In general, anything that involves hands-on interaction instead of merely question-and-answer (QA), and anything that allows kids to express themselves in a comfortable setting is best. In this chapter, we'll address research techniques to use with kids of different ages. While this isn't a "how-to" on user research, it will give you the tools you need to get data to inform and improve the experiences you're architecting. The following are some general guidelines for testing with kids (and adults!) of all ages.

---

1 Mike Kuniavsky, *Observing the User Experience* (San Francisco, CA: Morgan Kauffman Publishers, 2003).

2 Leah Buley, *The User Experience Team of One* (Brooklyn, NY: Rosenfeld Media, LLC, 2013).

Keep It Moving

Nobody likes trying to complete the same task over and over again. If kids aren't able to do what you ask them to do, or aren't answering the question you're trying to ask, move on to the next task or question. Think of another way to get the information you need instead of asking them to try the same thing repeatedly. My general rule of thumb for this is if the participant can't complete a task within two tries, move on. This approach will not only help move the session along, but it will also help ensure that you get meaningful data, because your participant will be interested and engaged throughout.

Let Them Lead

Instead of a moderator, think of yourself as a student. You need your participants to teach you about whether or not your hypotheses are correct. Whether you're conducting preliminary research before starting a design project or testing an existing interface, make it clear that the participants (aka children) are in the lead. When you ask probative questions, make sure they are open-ended and conversational, and let the kids feel as though they are in control. When you need clarification on a particular behavior, ask as an interested observer, not as a research facilitator. It takes practice to feel comfortable giving up this control, but it will yield much better and truer results.

Once when I was conducting a research study on virtual worlds, I worked with a little girl who struggled with everything I asked her. She was about 7 years old, and, like many kids of this age, was really nervous about getting something wrong. At one point, she looked over my shoulder and saw the enormous whiteboard and colorful markers on the wall behind me. She interrupted me mid-sentence and asked if she could draw on the whiteboard. Since we weren't getting anywhere with the activities I had planned, I told her she could. She went over to the board and proceeded to draw out her ideas for a virtual world, and they were amazingly insightful and revealing. I learned more about her perceptions on virtual worlds from her drawings than I would have from the computer tasks I initially wanted her to complete. Letting her take the lead and share her ideas in her own way helped drive and flesh out some key user needs.

> A great technique for conducting research with kids is the "master-apprentice" model. In this approach, the child serves as the master craftsman and the researcher represents the apprentice trying to learn the craft through observation and questioning. When using this model, make sure you position your participant as the expert at the very beginning of the session. Encourage her to teach you as you watch and listen.

Provide Closure

If a child is halfway through an activity when the session ends, let him finish up. If he has tried to complete a task twice unsuccessfully, show him how to do it and then ask how it could be clearer or easier. If a kid is very engrossed in a design project, either work with that child to finish it or give it to him to take home and finish on his own. Typically, when conducting task-based testing with adults, researchers let participants move onto the next task without demonstrating the right way to complete the one on which they were not successful. Kids have a hard time with this, especially 6–8s. Providing this closure and completion for them is important.

Have an Agenda

As with adults, kids like to know what they'll be doing as part of a research session, especially if the session is one-on-one. Make sure that you explain every activity you'll be doing, and, more importantly, why you'll be doing it. For example, you might say something like, "We're going to look at some apps on an iPad today. I'd like you to show me how they work. I'll probably have lots of questions for you! Then we'll talk a little bit about the different things you do on the computer, and then we'll go find your mom."

Be Honest

Be clear about the purpose of the research. Make sure that the kids know they're not being tested, but that they're helping you make sites and apps for kids better. If you're in a lab, take them on a tour of the facility, and if you've got observers watching from a control room, bring the kids around to meet them. They'll love to see the equipment setup and will feel very important when they see that they'll be observed.

What You Need to Know About Informed Consent

As design researchers using human subjects, we're held to the same ethical principles and guidelines as other scientific fields testing products and information with people. As a result, we need to make sure our users consent in writing to participate in our research. If you've conducted any type of research in the past, you most likely have experience with release forms, but if you haven't conducted research with kids, you'll need to understand what's required in terms of informed consent.

TIP FOR MORE INFORMATION ON REGS

> If you are unsure about the U.S. Federal Regulations for human subject testing, the Online Ethics Center for Engineering and Science has some great resources. Visit www.onlineethics.org for information.

In the United States, kids under 18 are not allowed to consent on their own to participate in research. Research release forms *have* to be signed by a parent or legal guardian. When creating your consent form, use plain language (keep those pesky lawyers away, if you can) and review it line by line with the parent to make sure they understand. If you're using live sites or apps that require any Personally Identifiable Information, plan to use dummy data and include somewhere in the release form that kids will not be expected to use their own information. If you're going to be recording the session, make sure that parents know how and where the recordings are going to be used. For example, if you're going to be making a highlights reel and showing it to clients, that needs to be in the release form. And, like with any type of research, no consent form means *no participation.*

Figure 9.1 shows an example of a consent form for parents.

<PROJECT NAME>

INTRODUCTION

Your child has been invited to join a research study to investigate/test/compare/evaluate <insert purpose of study.> We are doing this research to learn <insert study goals.> Your child's data will be used along with data from other children. We will not store any personally identifiable information from your child and will not share results from the study that identify your child in any way.

WHAT IS INVOLVED IN THE STUDY?

Your child will be asked to <insert tasks or activities.> This will take about <insert time> minutes.

Your child can stop participating at any time.

DIGITAL RECORDING (if you plan on recording the sessions)

We would like to make a digital video and/or audio recording of your child during the session. This recording will be used only for research purposes and will not be shared publicly. A limited number of individuals will have access to this recording. These include:

<insert list of individuals—by role only—who will view the recording>

HONORARIUM

Your child will receive <insert honorarium> for his/her participation.

PERMISSION FOR A CHILD TO PARTICIPATE IN RESEARCH

As parent or legal guardian, I authorize <child's name> to participate in the research study described above.

Child's Name: _____

Child's Date of Birth: _____   _____

Parent or Legal Guardian's Name: _____

Parent or Legal Guardian's Signature: _____

Date _____

Researcher Signature: _____

<AFTER THE PARENT SIGNS, MAKE A COPY FOR THEM>

FIGURE 9.1

A sample consent form for parents to fill out.

Recruiting Kids as Participants

Perhaps the most challenging aspect of conducting research with kids is finding them. Parents are rarely eager to have people they don't know come to their homes and observe their kids, and are only slightly more comfortable at the prospect of taking their kids to a lab so they can be studied. I have had success reaching out to local schools and daycare centers and asking about the possibility of working with individual kids or small groups, and most of the time they're very accommodating, as long as parents are informed. You'll want to make sure that you contact schools in different demographic areas to make sure you have a broad sample of kids represented. It's usually a good idea to have an even number of girls and boys, unless you are working on a design specifically geared toward a specific gender. If that's the case, you'll want to focus your recruitment efforts on kids of that gender.

Another good way to recruit participants is to get in touch with local colleges or universities with child-development programs. Many of these have on-site preschools, and the fact that these are associated with an educational institution makes parents a little more comfortable with research activities.

TIP REWARDS AND STIPENDS

Make sure that you offer stipends to child participants that are comparable to those you'd offer adults; for example, if you normally pay a $100 honorarium, give the kids a gift card in the same amount. It's also nice to make them little "goodie bags" with stuff from the dollar store to provide immediate gratification. And always make sure that you give the gift card to the parents, as kids tend to lose or misplace them.

Researching with the Littlest Users

If you have the opportunity to conduct user research with 2–6-year-olds, you're in for a tough, but interesting time. The best research techniques to use with this group are ones that feel like play, but allow for direct observation.

Child-Parent Sessions

Kids in this age range tend to feel more confident in sharing their thoughts when a trusted adult is around, so you'll want to include parents or caregivers in the research, even if they're just observers. Parents can provide reassurance and encouragement and can help "translate" for you if you're not sure what the child is trying to say.

You can use pretty much any research technique in child-parent sessions, but you'll need to brief parents ahead of time in terms of the level of engagement you want from them. Some parents will be very concerned that their child should provide the "right" answer, and may even try to feed responses to the child, so you'll need to explain clearly that all answers are right, and that their child is giving you valuable data with everything he says or does. Some parents will want to "help" you by repeating the questions you ask in different ways so the child will understand. As well-meaning as these parents are, rewording the questions can provide leading information, so tell the parents before the session starts that they can prompt their child to answer, but they shouldn't rephrase your questions. This is going to be very hard for some parents, so you'll want to acknowledge and empathize at the outset.

PARENTS ARE USERS, TOO

Sometimes, no matter how hard you try or how well you communicate, parents will still feel the need to take control of the research during a parent-child session by interrupting, rephrasing your questions, or "translating" their child's ideas for you. In my experience, these parents tend to be younger, professional, and intense, with children who can't quite express themselves verbally yet.

To address this issue, try making parents perform the job of research assistants rather than participants. Ask them to lead certain activities, fetch toys and props, and ask for their opinions and insights. And always praise their child's creativity, intelligence, and fine motor skills. Once parents see that you think highly of their child, they'll relax and go with the flow.

Research Techniques

Since kids in this age group are just beginning to think abstractly, it's going to be hard to get data using techniques that require them to think through hypothetical situations. Your best bet is direct observation, preferably at the child's home, in comfortable surroundings. You don't have to observe actual digital interaction, but make sure that you have an opportunity to watch the child play.

Interviews

Before starting the observation, it's a good idea to get the child (and parent) comfortable with you and what you're planning to do. Like adults, kids enjoy talking about themselves and their interests. Introduce yourself, explain that you need their help in making computers fun for kids, and ask them basic questions, like "What's your favorite book?" and "What TV shows do you like?" It's OK if the parent prompts a little at this point, as the goal here is just to orient the kids and get them to see you as a friend. You can even offer information about yourself during this time, like what your favorite toys were when you were little, or how many brothers and sisters you have.

It's best not to take notes during this time, as both parent and child will worry that you're evaluating them. If you have an observer/note-taker with you, that person can be part of the conversation. If you have a release form for the parent to sign, you can record the session, but keep the recording device as small and hidden as possible, as it will distract the child from what you'd like her to do.

Contextual Inquiry

If you're in the child's home, ask her to show you her toys. Watch how she plays; does she go immediately for the ones that make noise and move around? Or does she show you a favorite doll or plush animal? See how long she spends with each toy, and whether she spends more time with toys that provide a response, or the ones she has to "speak" for. You can ask specific questions during this time, like "What happens when you push the button?" or "What does your elephant like to eat?" This will help you determine if the child is more interested in imaginative play or bells-and-whistles. It may take awhile for you to figure this out, simply because kids in this age group move quickly among activities, but you should be able to gauge which ones are more engaging to the child.

The data you'll get from this type of research is an understanding of how to structure your site or app and what type of activities to include. Do your users prefer free play, or do they like structured action-response games?

Lab Research

If you're conducting research in a lab setting, you'll need to get a bunch of age-appropriate toys. Instruments, crayons and paper, baby dolls, and blocks work well. You'll also want to have a computer or tablet in the room. Encourage the same sort of open exploration as you would in a home setting, and watch for the same types of interaction. It will take a little longer in a lab setting for kids to orient themselves to the available items, but with some encouragement from you and from their parents, they'll quickly warm up to the environment.

> **TIP** LIMIT GROUP ACTIVITIES WITH YOUNGER KIDS
>
> I don't recommend group research activities for this age group, as these younger kids are a little too egocentric to play cooperatively in this setting. If you must do group research, see if you can limit the group activities to the observational components and conduct the interviews individually.

Researching with the Control Freaks

Our wonderful 6–8s, believe it or not, are the easiest group to test with. If you give them plenty of up-front information in terms of what you're doing and why, they'll quickly warm up and jump into any type of activity you have planned. These guys are a little less willing to volunteer personal information, however, so you'll want to frame your questions a little bit differently with this group. The 6–8s work really well in friend or peer groups, particularly when you select a group of kids who know each other. This age group is also good at one-on-one sessions, and they are articulate enough to communicate their thoughts both verbally and creatively.

Get 'em Talking

Interviews, conducted alongside hands-on techniques, work great with this group. They love to tell stories about the things they do online or on their mobile devices, and will happily volunteer information about their favorite games, sites, and activities. When starting out, ask some general, easy questions about their computer use, when and where they use smartphones or tablets, and what TV shows they like to watch. It's also a good idea at this point to ask about any rules their parents have for computer use, and to find out how they feel about these rules. This will help them feel comfortable with the interview protocol and get their ideas flowing.

These kids will be less forthcoming about sites they don't like, so you may have to turn the tables on them a bit and use that most dreaded term *babyish*. For example, "What are some apps or sites that you feel are babyish or good for younger kids?" If you pick up any reluctance to share information, take the emphasis off the child and ask questions about friends and family members, such as "What is your best friend's favorite thing to do online?" or "What games does your older brother like?"

As we discussed earlier, you'll want to make these kids feel like the experts, so let them teach you. This tactic is especially important for this age group, as they are very concerned about what others think of them. In a non-patronizing way, ask questions that demonstrate a specific lack of knowledge on your part, like, "I don't really know a whole lot about the types of sites kids in second grade like. Can you tell me about some of them?" or "I've played *Angry Birds* before, but what are some other popular iPad games?" Be careful here, though, because if you play too dumb, these kids will see right through it and become distrustful of you.

Limit your interviews to 15 minutes or less. These kids get bored quickly and will start giving you one-word answers, which are quite unhelpful.

Channel Your Inner Indiana Jones

Professor Indiana Jones instilled the love of exploration and adventure in his students, and if you do the same, you'll get some great data. Conduct one-on-one open exploration sessions, where you invite your participants to openly explore sites and apps with little to no direction on your part. Have your participants explain everything they do. This will take some prompting, as these kids are nervous about doing anything wrong, but once you get them talking, you'll be in good shape. If they fall silent, point to elements on the screen and say stuff like, "Oh, what's that? What do you think will happen when you click on it?" If they find an activity they like, let them play it for as long as they want, and watch how their behavior changes as they move from novice to intermediate to expert. (Unlike usability testing, where you'll want kids to move on to the next activity after two tries, you'll want kids to self-direct during exploratory research.)

During exploration sessions, pay attention to the types of activities the kids spend the most time on, their body language when they find something they really like doing (Do they sit up straighter? Get closer to the device? Wiggle around more?), and their facial expressions. If they have trouble explaining what they like best about the activity, you can ask them things like, "How would you describe this to your mom?" or "What do you think your best friend would like about this?" This will help highlight the most important aspects of the experience and will give you actionable feedback to use when designing your product.

Bring Out the Crayons

In my experience, the best way to get information on designing for 6–8-year olds is to hold participatory design sessions. These work best when you use friend groups—groups of three or four school pals or neighborhood kids—because you'll be able to jump right in to the activity and avoid the whole getting-to-know-you phase. Gather the group at a large table that's covered with art supplies. (I like crayons, colored pencils, markers, modeling clay, and, of course, tons of blank paper.) Then give them a specific design task to accomplish together that's focused on what you want to learn. For example, when I did preliminary research for the *Planet Orange* site, we got a group of kids together and asked them to create things they'd want to have on a spaceship. We got everything from lava lamps to robotic dogs to super telescopes. We used this data to develop the items the kids could "purchase" with the money they earned on the site.

If you're developing an app, print out a whole bunch of blank iPad/iPhone/Android templates and let the kids draw or model right on them. Having the constraint of the template will help them frame their thoughts about the things they'd like to see on the screen and how they prefer to navigate through a mobile experience. You'll probably need to encourage them to work together, or at least to talk through some of their ideas, and you may need to ask some follow-up questions to get the ideas flowing, but once they get started, the momentum will continue.

Some of the stuff these kids will come up with during these sessions will be either impossible, ridiculous, or make no sense at all, but it will give you an idea of how they conceptualize information, how they prioritize features, and what they really believe would be fun.

A technique I love to use with the 6–8s is something I call "exploration centers." This idea came from my friend and colleague, Jon Ashley, who uses it when leading youth activities at his church. This technique breaks up the research into manageable activities, keeps the kids from getting bored, and provides additional opportunities for observation. It does require at least two other adults, one preferably a researcher. To conduct exploration centers, you should set up activities in different rooms. For example, one room could be for interviews, one room could be for computer/mobile activities, one could be for participatory design, and one could be for "break time." Bring in a group of friends (no more than five, or things will get backed up) and rotate the kids through the rooms, finishing up with all of them in the participatory design room where they work together. Each activity should last between 15 and 20 minutes. In the break room, provide snacks and juice, as well as games, puzzles, art supplies, and videos. Have someone in the room observing the kids and noting which activities they choose to do. This backup will help provide a little more context around the kids' preferences in an offline environment.

Researching with the Experts

Kids ages 8–12 can be challenging during research sessions. They're concerned about what you think of them, and, as a result, tend to volunteer less information and give single-word, monotone answers to your questions. They're less interested in impressing you with their knowledge and more interested in whether or not you think they're cool. This can result in expressionless responses and bored, disinterested body language. We've all been there. You need to be patient, focused, and treat them as you would an adult participant.

Stick to One-on-Ones

Much like the younger 2–4s, the 8–12s do better in one-on-one settings. If you're designing for the younger end of this group, 8- and 9-year-olds, you may be able to get away with some group exercises, but for the most part, these kids get impatient when the conversation or activity doesn't progress as they'd like, and this causes them to disengage. You can adjust one-on-one sessions to the participant's level of interest much more easily.

When conducting in-depth interviews, start out as you would when interviewing adults, asking basic questions first and moving to the more personal, complicated ones after the participant feels comfortable. Again, it's very important not to talk down to these kids, or to even make them feel like they're kids, because they're trying so hard to seem grown up. Don't be afraid to ask these guys the harder, more abstract questions, like "What kinds of things might you lie about online?" or "What impact do your friends have on what games you like?" They'll usually answer honestly, especially if you keep the tone conversational and let them do most of the talking. Defer to their knowledge and expertise.

Go Back to School

A great way to get qualitative data from 8–12s is to visit/observe them in school settings. Reach out to local middle schools and see if there's a teacher or class you can connect with and observe. This will give you great insight into how kids interact offline with educational material. Do they respond better to hands-on learning activities, or do they like to absorb information and reinforce the learning by taking notes and asking questions? You'll notice differences here across personality and gender, but you'll be able to see patterns pretty quickly. Also, some teachers are better than others, and all teachers have different styles, so see if you can observe four or five classes from different schools (an urban, a suburban, a private, and a charter are good choices) to get more comprehensive data.

After you observe classes, see if you can pull some of the kids aside for one-on-one interviews. Ask about their thoughts about school, their favorite aspects, subjects, friends, and so on. These pre-teens have probably started using social media, so ask about how their online activities map to their offline friendships. You'll get some important insights into how they view relationships, technology, education, and media. And being in a school setting makes everything feel a little safer to them, since your presence is sanctioned by "the powers that be."

Lab Testing

These young folks are great in a traditional, lab-based usability-test setting. They'll be curious about the two-way mirror, if you're in a standard lab, so give them a tour and introduce them to any observers you may have. Explain that the observers are helping you out by taking notes on the important things the kids are doing, and that they need the kids to be honest and open with their thoughts and ideas.

When you're in the lab, give them specific tasks to accomplish, just as you would when conducting usability testing with adults. Ask them to talk aloud and describe what they're thinking and doing. It's important to note that these pre-teens aren't great at talking about themselves, so you'll have to prompt and prod gently during the sessions.

TIP PROVIDE REASSURANCE

In my experience, 8–12-year-olds talk softly and get embarrassed easily, so you'll need to do a little more reassuring with them than you might for younger kids or adults. When something engages them, see if you can pinpoint exactly what and why. Again—and I can't stress this enough—don't treat them like kids, or ask them questions like "What would kids do here?" This isn't about kids in general, it's about them, and the emphasis should be on the research, not on the fact that what you're researching is "for kids."

Surveys

Since these children are able to read and write confidently, surveys are a great way to get specific information that they might be less comfortable sharing in person. Make the surveys anonymous, but you can ask for information like age and gender.

Using surveys will get you some quantitative data to balance your qualitative work, but using surveys alone won't give you the full story, especially with kids. You can distribute surveys to kids in classrooms after you conduct your observational studies, but again, what kids think and what kids say they think are different. You can also ask children to complete a brief survey either before or after (or both) a lab study to measure attitudes and behavior against the behaviors you observe.

When crafting your surveys, use a combination of multiple-choice and free-form questions. It's a good idea to provide four choices for each multiple-choice question instead of five, which is the norm for adults. Children are pretty savvy when it comes to multiple-choice tests, and if they feel they might be evaluated on their answers (which they will, even if the surveys are anonymous), they'll check the neutral center choice every time. My recommendation is to use a scale of 1–4, with 1 being "disagree," 2 being "sort of disagree," 3 being "sort of agree," and 4 being "agree." Kids will respond to this casual language and feel less worried about picking the "right" answer. And since you're not providing a "neither agree nor disagree" choice, you won't get a bunch of useless neutral data.

Chapter Checklist

Here's a checklist to help you review the information from Chapter 9. In the next chapter, we'll take a hands-on look at designing apps for kids of different ages.

When conducting design research with kids, you'll want to do the following:

- ☐ Use hands-on activities so kids can show you what they think instead of just telling you.

- ☐ Let kids be the experts and guide the session, using the "master-apprentice" approach.

- ☐ Tailor your research activities to the specific age group you're designing for.

- ☐ Let the goals of your experience determine what research activities, tools, and stimuli you use.

- ☐ Help parents feel part of the process, especially for younger kids.

- ☐ Create an informed consent form for parents to sign.

Catalina N. Bock

User Experience Researcher, YouTube, Google

 *With degrees in both user experience design and research, **Catalina N. Bock** has collaborated with multiple creative teams in companies across the U.S., Europe, Canada, and South America in the area of user-centered product development with a focus on children and youth.*

Catalina currently works at Google, as a user experience researcher for YouTube. Previous professional engagements included LEGO, Intel, Nickelodeon, and Yahoo. Catalina is the author of multiple articles and talks on the user experience field, and she is also an advisor at Stanford University and the California College of the Arts.

DLG: You've done a lot of work in the field of research and design for children. What would you say is the most important thing to remember when conducting UX research with kids under the age of 12?

CNB: I'd say the most important thing is, you need to have a great deal of flexibility and patience. It's hard to predict how the research activities are going to go. You may find out what you planned to do isn't giving you the kind of data you need, so you have to be able to change your process and methodology as you go. You may find that it's hard to build rapport with kids, or to get them to talk, and you may need to involve parents or teachers in the process. You can plan to involve parents in certain ways, but that may affect the responses you get from kids, so you need to be open minded and aware of the situation.

Additionally, and depending on the complexity of the research activity, you might need to prepare activities such as games, workbooks, and drawing sheets to serve as a stimuli during your sessions. These can take time to prepare and might not work the way you thought once you use them with kids. You will definitely want to do a pilot session or two to test the waters and see if your assumptions about the research methods will work. If the methods don't work and you see you're not able to get the kind of data you need, you may have to come up with a different approach.

DLG: We know that designing for a 2-year-old is very different than designing for a 12-year-old. The same is true for research as well. What are the key differences in researching with kids of different age groups?

CNB: The 2–4-year-olds are just starting to develop cognitive and linguistic skills. They're unable to express themselves clearly using words, so you'll need to use hands-on activities to understand how they think and behave. Observe them in a natural environment, like home or school, so you can see the materials that they use on a daily basis. I recommend conducting observational studies without parents initially, so you have a less-biased environment, but once you start asking questions or asking them to do things, you'll need participation from parents and teachers to provide some context about the child's reactions to the things you're observing.

Starting at around age 5 or 6, kids are more vocal and can explain context and tell stories about what they do. This makes them easier to understand, so you can incorporate some interview questions into the research. You start seeing a big difference between girls and boys at this age. Girls can relax and sit still for longer time periods, while boys want to be more active and activity-focused. You'll need to create sessions that are very involved, with lots of different activities to keep them interested.

With 8–10-year-olds, if your interface is not too complex, you can do paper prototype testing. This tends to work better with touch interfaces than with click interfaces. You can have them build their own paper prototype as part of a participatory design activity, or you can conduct a concept evaluation test with a paper prototype that you created, which might uncover early usability issues.

It's important to remember that kids' short attention spans last until the teenage years. Keep sessions an hour or less, unless you're working with older kids who are super-passionate about the project.

One thing that's really important when researching with kids of all ages is parental approval, on some level. You want to find out the kind of apps and sites they like their kids to play with, how much they expect to pay, etc. Even though you want the product to be primarily kid-focused, it's important to find out if the parent approves, since they're the ones who will ultimately be buying it.

DLG: You mentioned participatory design. What are the benefits of conducting participatory design sessions with kids? Is there a particular age range that works best for participatory design activities?

CNB: Participatory design works best with older kids. What's great about it is you involve users as experts on the products they use regularly to help with the design process. It's used a lot for creating ideal, future experiences for kids and adults. You're not trying so much to see if they can use the app or find a specific button. It's more about discovery, about engaging kids to generate new ideas. I did this a lot when I worked at LEGO, and it was very compelling.

It's important to note that the main goal of participatory design is not to come up with the next generation of a product during the sessions, but about getting to see the world through the kids' eyes. What I love about it is that I'm creating with them, I'm getting my hands dirty, I'm watching them play with Play-Doh and listening to their stories, hearing them imagining how things could be. This type of activity can open your eyes and challenge your assumptions—you expect kids to respond in a certain way and just by watching and listening and seeing how they create things, you can get rid of these assumptions and get a true picture. Once you get their creative juices flowing, you get to see things you haven't thought of before.

In my experience, participatory design is best with kids 6–12. They have the basic motor and linguistic skills. They're creative and very eager to participate and help design. They love creating collages, kids' versions of mind maps, etc. They're generally very excited to participate. With younger kids, it's more challenging because of their cognitive and language skills, and older kids are sometimes "too cool" to participate.

One thing that's very important is to provide very clear expectations for both kids and parents. At LEGO, I did a lot of this type of research with kids. The kids were excited to participate, but they really expected that their ideas would be implemented as actual products. You need to tell them that their ideas are awesome, but may not actually be developed exactly as they're saying, that their ideas could be the foundation of a product, but will likely go through many iterations and may be transformed a lot. You have to listen and be excited to hear their ideas, within reason. Kids get sad when they hear their product ideas might not be created, so you have to manage it so their feelings don't get hurt.

The same is true with parents. Sometimes they want to know what their kids will be getting in exchange for their ideas; for example, if their kid comes up with the next big thing, will they get paid for it? It's important to tell them that the kids will get a stipend for their participation, but that ideas go through many rounds and often end up in a different direction.

DLG: What are some good ways to recruit kids for research sessions?

CNB: It really depends on the product and the company. If you're working with a big company that does a lot of work with kids, it may have a database of potential participants. You can also do a traditional screening process where you post a survey online and recruit from there—parents will complete the survey on behalf of their kids. Once you have a pool of participants, it's great to call them or do a follow-up with the kids to make sure they can express themselves verbally and to find out a little more about them before you bring them in to participate.

I've also had to do more guerilla-style recruiting. You can reach out to daycares and schools, or talk to friends and family members who have kids in the right demographic. I also know people who have gone to parks or museums and recruited from there. When I work with startups or do an app for myself, I use friends and family. For example, a friend with a 5-year-old can introduce you to other families with 5-year-olds as well. ■

SOPHIA

CHAPTER 10

An App for All Ages

Samantha, Age 5
A card for Samantha's friend, Sophia.

We want to encourage a world of creators, of inventors, of contributors. Because this world that we live in, this interactive world, is ours.

—Ayah Bdeir

In this section, we'll put everything you've learned into practice and take a look at how to design an app that works for each individual age group. I've created a series of high-fidelity wireframes for a basic video app—since kids of all ages watch videos —to show you how designs should evolve along with kids' abilities.

Things to look for include the following:

- **Controls:** The number, type, and size of user controls changes as kids get older.

- **Choice:** The number of choices available increases to support kids' evolving content needs.

- **Simplicity:** The app remains relatively simple to use, even as we add more content and more functionality.

- **Hierarchy:** The levels of content hierarchy increase slightly for each age group.

- **Design Patterns:** Common design patterns start creeping into the app as kids reach the 6–8-year-old age group.

Same App, Different Ages?

You probably won't ever design a single app for kids from the ages of 2 through 12. As we've discussed throughout this book, a toddler's needs are very different from those of an older child when it comes to digital design. That being said, there are rare occasions—mostly in the form of "container" apps that house content or games—when a single experience must meet the needs of all users. Examples of these "container" apps include game console experiences, audio or music apps, and video players, which we'll see in greater detail later in this chapter.

If you do find yourself designing one of these container apps, and you don't want to ask your users to self-identify by age, you'll want to err on the side of over-the-top simplicity. Think about the Nintendo Wii hand controller. It has seven buttons, some very basic iconography, and no text, yet it allows people of all ages to play all different kinds of games. If the tasks your users need to perform require more complex controls, depending on the content they want to view or play, consider adding in levels from beginner to expert that users can choose based on what it is they want to do. You can increase the complexity of the controls based on the selected level. Always start at the beginner level so that the youngest kids don't have to choose. In addition to keeping younger users engaged, this approach has the added benefit of making older kids and more sophisticated users feel important, because they get to pick the "expert" path.

Please note, however, that even though we'll be looking at a video player app in this chapter, the goal here is to illustrate the differences in design patterns used for different age groups and not to show how to design a single app for kids of all ages.

2–4-Year-Olds

Let's start at the beginning, with our 2–4-year-olds (see Figure 10.1 and Table 10.1). Notice the large images, the simple scrubber, and the bold, but limited colors.

> **TIP** BEGIN AT THE BEGINNING
>
> Kids under 5 like to watch videos over and over and over again from start to finish. When designing for younger kids, make sure that videos in your app start at the beginning each time and play automatically. Older kids prefer continuity, so when designing for kids older than 6, have videos pick up where they left off.

PHOTO ATTRIBUTION: "KIDS PAINTING" BY JIM PENNUCCI IS LICENSED UNDER CC BY 2.0
DESIGN ICONS ©2014 SHELBY BERTSCH
WIREFRAME ICONS ©2014 MICHAEL ANGELES

FIGURE 10.1

A sample screen from our newly created video player for 2–4-year-olds.

TABLE 10.1 LANDING SCREEN FOR 2–4-YEAR-OLDS

ID	Section	Description
A	Color	Use a limited set of bright, bold colors. These colors should act as guides, identifying specific content and interactions. It's tempting to splash color all over the screen, especially for kids with short attention spans who can't read, but too many colors in them can cause these little guys to get overwhelmed, so they lose interest quickly.
B	Navigation	Keep your navigation simple. If you make navigation elements wiggle and make noise, kids won't realize they have another purpose other than to wiggle and make noise. It's natural to want to draw attention to navigation items by adding sounds and actions, but if you do so, your users won't understand they can touch them to watch different videos. You can use size and color intensity to highlight the video currently playing, but keep animation and sound to a minimum.
C	Icons	The 2–4-year-olds are not able to think abstractly, so avoid using icons and symbols, even ones that may seem completely intuitive. You can, however, start introducing some basic shapes that mimic items kids are familiar with in the physical world, such as arrows, stars, and "thumbs-up" signs. Using forward- and backward-pointing arrows to indicate the presence of additional video content will resonate with users at the older age of this range, say, $3^1/_2$- to 4-year-olds, but will likely be ignored by the littlest kids.
D	Video	For the record, as a user, I *hate* auto-play; however, when you are designing for kids under 4, auto-play is your friend. Make the steps between accessing the app and actually playing a video as few as possible, so kids can quickly understand the purpose of the app and start using it successfully. Also, make auto-play an option that parents can turn on and off in a parental controls area, but default to auto-play on install so kids can get the immediate gratification they're looking for.
E	Scrubber	Because kids this young don't really understand icons, all you need is a basic play/pause button and a scrolling timeline in case parents need to rewind or forward to specific parts. It's also nice to throw in a counter so parents can see how long certain videos are and how much is left to watch. Since kids get bored easily and usually don't watch videos to the end, you can hold off on adding full-screen functionality until your audience gets a little older. But kids should be able to switch quickly between videos instead of focusing on an immersive entertainment experience.
F	Volume	Kids may recognize this symbol and choose to ignore it, but parents will grasp for it frantically. Keep it prominently positioned as part of the video controls so that parents don't have to fumble with the device itself, and you'll get lots of happy parental reviews in the app store.

4–6-Year-Olds

Let's take a look at the same video player, but designed for a 4-to-6-year-old audience (see Figure 10.2 and Table 10.2). The same basic principles are at play here, with the addition of some subtle but important functionality:

PHOTO ATTRIBUTION: "KIDS PAINTING" BY JIM PENNUCCI IS LICENSED UNDER CC BY 2.0
ICONS ©2014 SHELBY BERTSCH
WIREFRAME ICONS ©2014 MICHAEL ANGELES

FIGURE 10.2

A sample landing screen from a video player for 4–6-year-olds.

TABLE 10.2 LANDING SCREEN FOR 4-6-YEAR-OLDS

ID	Section	Description
A	On-Screen Elements	While littler kids require larger targets and broader gestures, older kids' motor skills are better developed, and they can interact more easily with finer on-screen elements and smaller gestures. You can shrink navigational elements for these guys so you have more room for a larger content area and more detailed functionality.
B	Saving and Storing	The idea of permanence starts becoming important at this age. Give kids the opportunity to save their favorite videos so they can easily access them whenever they want. This functionality doesn't have to be complicated, but it should be personalized (first name is fine) and accessible from everywhere within the app.
C	Sequence	When kids are around age 4, narrative and flow become a bit more important to them, as they start understanding more complex scenarios. Younger children like abstract exploration, but these folks like sequential discovery. As a result, you may want to let kids seamlessly switch to the previous and next videos in the line-up without requiring them to remove themselves from the experience and go back up to the app navigation.
D	Auto-Play	You can turn off auto-play now. Kids from 4–6 like to have a little more control over their on-screen interactions, so allow them to choose when to play the video. A very simple "play" button in the middle of the video screen is all you need, as long as you have your standard play/pause functionality in the scrubber.
E	Favorites	When kids are this age, it will be important to give them the ability to save and store their favorite videos. A simple favorite selector, in the form of a heart or a plus sign, lets kids add items to their favorites menu. (I actually think the heart works better here, since kids understand that hearts mean love.)
F	Expand	Now's a good time to introduce the expand or full-screen view video player. Kids in this age range will appreciate a more immersive experience and will want to see things larger and in higher definition. Make sure there's an easy way for users to get back to the main screen—an unobtrusive back arrow works well—so they don't lose their sense of place.

Let's open up that Favorites view we've been talking about (see Figure 10.3 and Table 10.3).

TIP WHEN TO STOP USING AUTO-PLAY

Auto-playing videos (videos that play automatically when users open the app) are great for 2–4-year-olds, but become problematic as children get older. When kids hit age 4, they get startled and annoyed when videos play without their consent. Give older kids more control by letting them play videos on their own.

PHOTO ATTRIBUTION: "KIDS PAINTING" BY JIM PENNUCCI IS LICENSED UNDER CC BY 2.0
ICONS ©2014 SHELBY BERTSCH
WIREFRAME ICONS ©2014 MICHAEL ANGELES

FIGURE 10.3
"Favorites" window for 4–6-year-olds.

TABLE 10.3 FAVORITES SCREEN FOR 4-6-YEAR-OLDS

ID	Section	Description
A	Overlay	A simple, visual overlay or drop-down menu can hold the user's Favorites. Use this type of interaction judiciously with younger kids, because lots of windows opening or drawers popping up and down can quickly get annoying. Create a *tappable* element to open this overlay and make it extremely easy to close. (For example, if a user taps anywhere else on the screen other than in the overlay, the window can close.)
		Of course, tapping one of the video images in the overlay will open the video in the main content area. The overlay can close at this point as well.

6–8-Year-Olds

Now onto the 6–8-year-olds (see Figure 10.4 and Table 10.4). You'll notice a big jump in functionality and complexity here, simply because when kids start elementary school, they start learning more elaborate and complex concepts. They also start requiring a lot more up-front explanation, because, unlike younger kids, they are acutely aware of the difference between getting something right and getting something wrong. And they really, *really* don't want to get anything wrong.

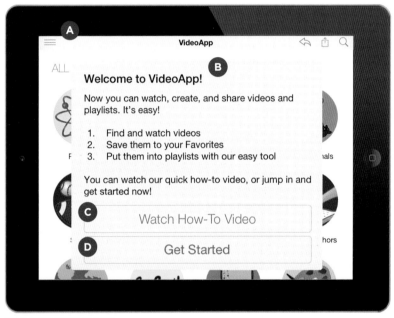

ICONS ©2014 SHELBY BERTSCH
WIREFRAME ICONS ©2014 MICHAEL ANGELES

FIGURE 10.4

Giving 6–8-year-olds an intro screen helps them figure out what to do.

TABLE 10.4 INTRO SCREEN FOR 6–8-YEAR-OLDS

ID	Section	Description
A	Navigation	You can introduce the standard mobile navigation bar at this age. While these kids are still wrestling with abstraction, they understand basic iconography and have most likely learned what the major mobile icons represent. Keep the functionality in this navigation bar as simple as you can, with as few options as possible, just to get kids familiar with this type of interaction. You can also use gestures as navigation here.
B	Instructions	Give these kids as much up-front instruction as they'll need to get started using the app. With these kids, as with adult audiences, you'll want to avoid superfluous content, but a basic overview of the app's goals, benefits, and first steps will be super-helpful for these guys. When they get a little older, they'll skip right over the instructions, but at this age, they'll read every word if it will make it less likely for them to make a mistake.
C	Content in Multiple Formats	When you're designing for kids 6–8, the older ones will know how to read, but the younger ones might not be completely proficient yet. It's a good idea with this age group to think about presenting instructional content in more than one format, for example, in text and in video, or through animation and audio. This ensures that regardless of their reading level, kids will understand what to do. Of course, if you are using text, keep words to 1 or 2 syllables as practical. If you use longer words, make sure that kids can easily sound them out.
D	Buttons	You should have no problems using *tappable* buttons with this age group. For overlay messages where there are multiple options, make sure these options are clear and distinct. For example, in this overlay, kids can choose between learning more or using the app: instruction versus use. Each choice will close the overlay.

After kids close the overlay, they should be able to engage with the content immediately. You can also begin using some of the same design patterns you use for adults with the 6–8s (see Figure 10.5 and Table 10.5.)

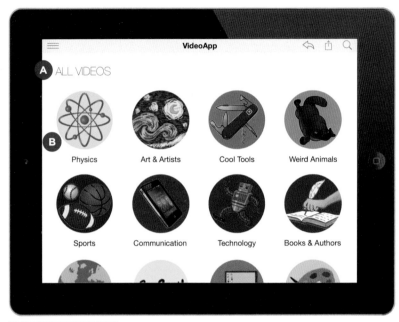

ICONS ©2014 SHELBY BERTSCH
WIREFRAME ICONS ©2014 MICHAEL ANGELES

FIGURE 10.5
You can start using common design patterns for 6–8-year-olds.

TABLE 10.5 LANDING SCREEN FOR 6–8-YEAR-OLDS

ID	Section	Description
A	Labeling	For 6–8s, you'll want to err on the side of overlabeling rather than underlabeling, simply because these kids want to know exactly what everything on the screen is or does, and how it should be used.
B	Symbols	These guys are starting to not only understand, but also to rely on abstract thinking to understand information and solve problems. It's a good idea, however, to combine an icon or a symbol with a corresponding text description so that kids can be extra-sure what they mean. Again, more information is better than less for this age group.

Once kids tap a specific video category, you can start introducing more complex functionality in terms of the player and video catalog (see Figure 10.6 and Table 10.6). Kids 6–8 will enjoy an interface that feels less "babyish," but it still needs to accommodate their cognitive level.

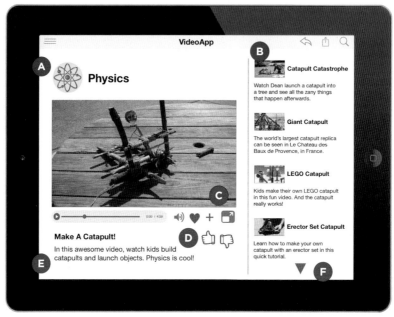

PHOTO ATTRIBUTIONS: "IMG_0405" BY ROY CHIJIIWA, "DEAN AND THE CATAPULT" BY REBECCA SIEGEL, "WEAPON OF MASS DISTRACTION" BY SALVA BARBERA, "LEGO CITY ADVENT CALENDAR – DAY 2" BY KENNY LOUIE, AND "LOADED AND READY" BY WINDELL OSKAY ARE LICENSED UNDER CC BY 2.0
ICONS ©2014 SHELBY BERTSCH
WIREFRAME ICONS ©2014 MICHAEL ANGELES

FIGURE 10.6

A video player for 6–8-year-olds that has enhanced saving and sharing features.

TABLE 10.6 VIDEO SCREEN FOR 6–8-YEAR-OLDS

ID	Section	Description
A	Consistency	Similar to designing for adults, when you design for these kids, you should carry over color/icon treatment whenever you reference a specific category, so the users have a sense of place and context. Try to avoid deep nesting of content, because these kids will get stuck and have a hard time figuring out where they are in the app. When they get a little older, you'll be able to introduce the concepts of nesting and cross-categorization.
B	Lists and Inventories	It's a good idea to let these kids see what other items (in this case, videos) live in the category they've selected. For littler ones, having a single item per category, or elevating individual items to the topmost level, works well, since they aren't great at classifying objects or information, but older kids like organization and structure, and can understand how objects are grouped. In this example, you can see all physics videos listed to the right of the player, so kids can easily jump from video to video in case they feel as though they picked the "wrong" one to watch.
C	Scrubber	You can add additional functionality to the scrubber, such as "add to playlist" and "expand screen." Kids are familiar with these concepts and will be able to successfully interpret and understand the standard icons.
D	Ratings	While these guys are a little young for traditional ratings and reviews (they get confused about where the ratings come from and why they should care), it's a good idea to let them share their opinion of a content item and to store it in the app. Here, the traditional "thumbs-up" and "thumbs-down" symbols let the kids rate the videos, so the next time the video appears in a list or in search results, they'll be able to recall how they felt about it.
E	Descriptions	These children like context, so you'll want to provide a brief description of each video. (If you can also supply voice-over audio for the descriptions, all the better.) If kids understand what they can expect to see in the videos, they'll feel more confident about choosing the "right" one to watch.
F	Off-Screen Content	The 6-year-olds are pretty confident with gestural interfaces, but you may want to throw in a scrolling indicator just to let them know there are additional videos below the ones shown on the screen. This will encourage them to swipe the screen to view more.

Slide-in menus are pretty effective for this group. It's also a good idea to include a menu icon or button in the navigation bar at the top so that it's easy for them to access the menu if they don't want to slide. Even though we're seeing trends away from these patterns when designing for adults, kids have learned what they are and how they're used, and look for them as app navigation.[1] Figure 10.7 show an example of a menu panel for 6–8-year-olds, and Table 10.7 highlights some important points to consider.

TIP LIMIT YOUR WIDGETS

Don't overdo it with widgets and icons for 6–8-year-olds. It will cause additional cognitive burdens for them and make them second-guess their actions. Focus on intuitive gestures and common design patterns to guide them through the experience instead of giving them complete control over every aspect of the interface.

WIREFRAME ICONS ©2014 MICHAEL ANGELES

FIGURE 10.7
A menu panel works well to help 6–8s find their place.

---

1 http://thenextweb.com/dd/2014/04/08/
ux-designers-side-drawer-navigation-costing-half-user-engagement/

TABLE 10.7   SLIDE-IN MENU FOR 6–8-YEAR-OLDS

ID	Section	Description
A	Search	Kids on the younger end of this age range probably won't use search functionality a whole lot, but older kids will, especially if there are videos they want to access right away. You can use simply a field and the search icon here, as these kids will know just what to do.
B	Navigation	Of course, you'll want to use the same category icons here as you do in the main content area. If you've got multiple types of content for kids to access, as shown here, you'll want to do some research to find out how they would like to organize these content types. Kids don't think like adults, and their classifications may differ from how you've anticipated organizing everything.
		Make sure that kids can get to everything they need from the menu panel. These guys will scroll to find what they're looking for. What they won't do is tap various buttons to find what they need. So while an adult audience might respond positively to multiple menu panels and different navigation options within the app, these kids will look for more of a "launch pad" type area where they can access everything.

8–10-Year-Olds

Now let's move to our 8-10-year-olds (see Figure 10.8). As you'll see, the gap between this app and one designed for an adult audience is narrowing (see Table 10.8).

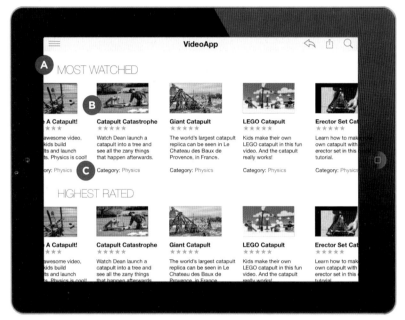

PHOTO ATTRIBUTIONS: "IMG_0405" BY ROY CHIJIIWA, "DEAN AND THE CATAPULT" BY REBECCA SIEGEL, "WEAPON OF MASS DISTRACTION" BY SALVA BARBERA, "LEGO CITY ADVENT CALENDAR – DAY 2" BY KENNY LOUIE, AND "LOADED AND READY" BY WINDELL OSKAY ARE LICENSED UNDER CC BY 2.0
ICONS ©2014 SHELBY BERTSCH
WIREFRAME ICONS ©2014 MICHAEL ANGELES

FIGURE 10.8
Let 8–10-year-olds jump right in, with little to no instruction.

TABLE 10.8 LANDING SCREEN FOR 8–10-YEAR-OLDS

ID	Section	Description
A	Dynamic Classification	Our 8–10s are incredibly curious about the world around them. Instead of reading instructions, they want to just jump right in and learn as they go. What seems to be compelling for these guys is to get a glimpse into what other users are doing within the interface. For example, with a video app, you might create dynamic categories such as "Most Watched" and "Highest Rated" that update regularly. Seeing new or refreshed content on the landing screen of an app, based on the behaviors of other kids like them, is pretty exciting for these kids, since it's not the same old stuff they've seen a million times. These kids may still gravitate toward the same group of videos each time, but they'll love to see how the content changes. In fact, a "New Stuff" category would be pretty cool here, too.
B	Description	These kids won't read descriptions as closely as the 6–8s, but they will scan for keywords of interest to decide if the video's worth watching or not. What will be especially important to these kids is the rating shown here. As mentioned earlier, the opinions of others are fascinating to them, so they'll use the ratings to determine whether or not they're interested in a particular video. Since kids of this age can understand nuances better than younger children, you can use a star rating or a numerical rating here to indicate popularity, as opposed to a like/dislike toggle like the thumbs-up, thumbs-down that was used with the younger guys.
C	Taxonomy	Just as these kids can understand multi-tiered ratings systems, they can also understand multi-tiered categorization. So, in addition to the "Most Watched" or "Highest Rated" classifications, which aren't permanent, you can introduce cross-classification here by placing a link to the content category the video lives in as well. For example, a 9-year-old will understand that a video appearing in the "Most Watched" section of this screen has a permanent "home" in the Physics category.

This page should look pretty familiar (see Figure 10.9); it's almost the same as the video screen you looked at for the 6–8s. There are a few marked differences, however, as shown in Table 10.9

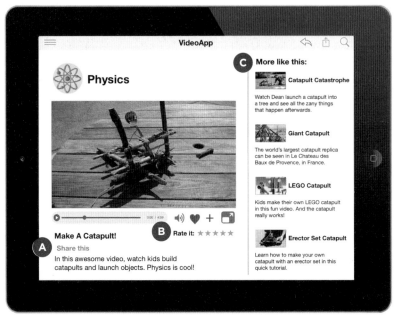

FIGURE 10.9

The 8–10s like to share and rate content.

TABLE 10.9 VIDEO SCREEN FOR 8–10-YEAR-OLDS

ID	Section	Description
A	Sharing	The 8–10s love the idea of being able to share something with their friends. Including this functionality will make the app feel more personal and extensible to these guys, especially if they can share stuff they made, like video mashups or playlists.
B	Ratings	We talked about the importance of ratings on the previous page, but here we're going to discuss the importance of contributing to ratings as well. Using a simple interactive rating feature, like tappable stars or numbers, will encourage kids to add their voice without a lot of work. It's best not to allow kids much younger than 12 to review products, media, or sites via a free-text field simply because you'll get a lot of expletives and useless single-word answers. If you want more detailed reviews, you can use a Q&A format with multiple-choice questions, but I'm not sure what the value will be in doing this, as kids (much like adults) are primarily interested in the rating itself.
C	Video List	For younger kids, showing a list of videos in the same content category works well here, because it gives them a sense of place and context. These older kids prefer a more personalized approach based on their own behaviors and needs. It's hard to do this well without a whole lot of data, but what you can do here, instead of only showing videos within the same content category, is to display videos similar to the one the user is watching. This lets kids feel as though they're seeing content curated for and by someone with similar ideas and interests.

Figure 10.10 shows the Add to Playlist functionality for the 8–10s. As you'll see, the playlist allows for self-expression, as well as the ability to organize content in a meaningful way. See Table 10.10 for a detailed overview of the elements on this screen.

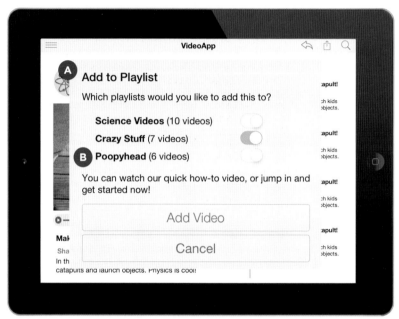

FIGURE 10.10
Add to Playlist functionality lets 8–10s be creative.

TABLE 10.10 "ADD TO PLAYLIST" SCREEN FOR 8–10-YEAR-OLDS

ID	Section	Description
A	Flow	While I don't recommend a lot of in-page interruptive messaging for younger kids (simply because it takes them out of the experience), providing subfunctionality within some sort of overlay or expandable panel works well for these guys, who are all over the place. When a user clicks the Add to Playlist button in the video player, it's okay to let him continue down this path via simple messaging and functionality. You can also let kids create a new playlist from this screen as well.
B	Self-Expression	These kids are at the age where they're starting to question authority and break the rules. My recommendation for this is to let them break the rules, within reason. If a user wants to name a playlist "Poopyhead," he should have the freedom to do this without much fanfare. Of course, you'll want to block any of the super-naughty words (and you can do this in a funny, engaging way), but silly and harmless self-expression is a good thing, even if it's slightly off-color.

Unlike our 6–8s, our 8–10s don't read instructions, and even if they do glance over them, they certainly don't follow them. As a result, you'll want to use your error messages to teach instead of relying on directions (see Figure 10.11 and Table 10.11).

PHOTO ATTRIBUTION: "IMG_0405" BY ROY CHIJIIWA IS LICENSED UNDER CC BY 2.0
WIREFRAME ICONS ©2014 MICHAEL ANGELES

FIGURE 10.11

Smart error messaging helps 8–10-year-olds learn how to use apps.

TABLE 10.11 ERROR MESSAGING FOR 8–10-YEAR-OLDS

ID	Section	Description
A	Error States	If you were designing this app for adults, on the previous screen you would probably not give users the option to add a video to a playlist that was already full. However, this will be distressing for kids in this age group, who most likely haven't read the instructions and will be worried when they don't see all their playlists on the screen. Since these kids learn by trial-and-error, your error messaging will have to serve double-duty, as both a notification and teaching tool. Keep messages friendly and upbeat, with specific information about what they did wrong and how to self-correct.
B	Fixing Mistakes	While it's important to use error messages to teach kids how to use your app, make sure this screen always provides a way to go back and correct the "mistake." In this case, give kids the option to edit the playlist they've chosen, so that they can remove a video from the playlist and then add the one they have selected.

We talked a little about how these kids like to share stuff with their friends. Now let's take a look at how to craft this functionality in a safe yet compelling way, as shown in Figure 10.12 and Table 10.12.

PHOTO ATTRIBUTION: "IMG_0405" BY ROY CHIJIIWA IS LICENSED UNDER CC BY 2.0
WIREFRAME ICONS ©2014 MICHAEL ANGELES

FIGURE 10.12
A simple sharing mechanism that is fun and safe.

TABLE 10.12   SHARING SCREEN FOR 8–10-YEAR-OLDS

ID	Section	Description
A	Form Design	Keep the form as simple and as basic as possible. These kids are probably pretty proficient with a tablet or mobile keyboard, but you want to limit the amount of typing they have to do since it can be pretty frustrating to enter data on a mobile device.
B	Contacts	You can let these kids share content via email or a text message. Many kids in this age range don't have email accounts, but they do have the ability to text via a mobile phone or an iPod Touch. Whatever mechanism you use, you'll want to limit the people a child can share with to the device's contact list. This reduces the possibility that these kids will contact someone they don't know by mistake and unknowingly share personal information with them.
C	Subject	To reduce the amount of data entry kids have to do, you can pre-populate this field with a generic subject, such as "A Video for You." Of course, if you're using an MMS service to send the message, you won't even need a subject line.
D	Message	Pre-populating this area is a good idea. Kids may not have anything to add to it, and may just be interested in sharing the video and moving on to the next one.

10–12-Year-Olds

Now let's look at a screen for a 10–12-year-old audience. These kids are pretty sophisticated app users, with cognitive abilities close to those of adults; as a result, you can do lots of interesting things here with labels, navigation, organizational structure, and content strategy. We're not going to go too deeply with this age group, but we are going to look at a landing screen construct (see Figure 10.13 and Table 10.13).

TIP PROVIDE CHOICE AND EXPLORATION

Although an app you design for 10–12-year-olds may look a lot like an app you would design for adults, you still want to be mindful of their unique cognitive, developmental, and emotional stages. Provide the right level of choice and exploration, and let kids hone in and personalize it to their specific areas of interest. (See Chapter 8 for more information.)

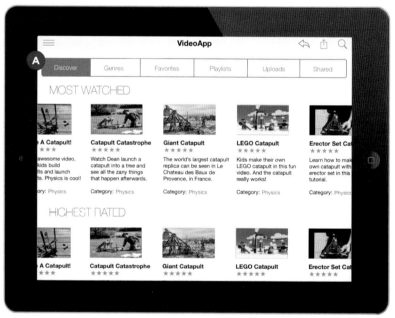

PHOTO ATTRIBUTIONS: "IMG_0405" BY ROY CHIJIIWA, "DEAN AND THE CATAPULT" BY REBECCA SIEGEL, "WEAPON OF MASS DISTRACTION" BY SALVA BARBERA, "LEGO CITY ADVENT CALENDAR - DAY 2" BY KENNY LOUIE, AND "LOADED AND READY" BY WINDELL OSKAY ARE LICENSED UNDER CC BY 2.0

ICONS ©2014 SHELBY BERTSCH

WIREFRAME ICONS ©2014 MICHAEL ANGELES

FIGURE 10.13

A successful app for 10–12-year-olds has a robust content strategy and hierarchy.

TABLE 10.13 LANDING SCREEN FOR 10–12-YEAR-OLDS

ID	Section	Description
A	Content Strategy	You can create a more detailed and complex hierarchy for these kids, which will allow you to add significantly more content than you could for younger ones. Creating another content level at the top lets you get more videos in front of users sooner, while still preserving a meaningful categorization. You can also combine personal content structure and a system hierarchy in this top level as well. This structure helps kids feel as though the app is more personal and more useful in meeting their needs.

Chapter Checklist

When developing apps for kids in specific age groups, make sure that you take the following areas into consideration.

Does your design cover the following areas?

☐ Use auto-play only for users younger than age 4?

☐ Give kids the right level of functionality for their age?

- 2–4-year-olds—Simple scrubber and playback control

- 4–6-year-olds—The ability to store favorites

- 6–8-year-olds—Saving and sharing

- 8–10-year-olds—Ratings and reviews, playlists

- 10–12-year-olds—Complex navigation, sorting, and filtering

☐ Develop a messaging strategy that maps to how kids learn?

☐ Provide either up-front instructions or follow-up information, depending on the age and cognitive level you're designing for?

Putting It All Together

Audrea, Age 7

T his chapter contains a series of checklists to guide you in your efforts to create the next great digital children's product. It draws on everything we've covered in the previous chapters, but focuses primarily on what you need to do to get your site live or your app launched. These lists will help you make sure that you cover "the basics," so that your time and energy will go into practicing all the techniques you learned in previous chapters.

First, the Questions

Our first set of checklists is designed to make sure that you understand the why, who, and what of your site or app by answering a few questions. These are important, especially if you're designing an app, because platform app stores frequently need this information.

Why?

- Why do you want to create this site or app?

- What are your goals in creating it? Financial? Other?

- What do you hope kids who use your product will come away with?

- How would you like kids to describe it to their friends?

- What similar products are available currently and how will yours be different?

- What's your product's "elevator pitch?" Does it cover all of the above?

> **NOTE** ELEVATOR PITCH
>
> An elevator pitch is a short (less than one minute) speech that describes the most important aspects of your product. Good elevator pitches focus on the product's goals, audience, and unique value proposition, as well as the product's target users and a brief overview of the functionality. Audrey Watters wrote a great article for readwrite.com called "The Art of the Elevator Pitch" with some excellent tips for creating your perfect pitch.[1]

---

1 http://rfld.me/1n2cKn4

Who?

- Who is your product for?

- What age/interests/activities are you targeting?

- What are the cognitive, physical, and technical skills of the kids you're designing for?

- What emotions or responses are you hoping to evoke?

- What do your users' parents expect from your design? What's their PTR?

- How do you envision kids using your product? Alone? With peers? With a parent, peer, or teacher?

NOTE PTR (PARENTAL THRESHHOLD FOR THE REVOLTING)

As discussed in Chapter 2, the PTR is the fine line between a site or app that is acceptable to a parent, as opposed to one that is too over-the-top in terms of content, imagery, or activities.

What?

- What channels fit your design (Web, responsive, mobile, other)?

- What are the main tasks or activities that kids will be able to perform?

- How will it work? What features and functionality will it include?

- Is the product a game? What opportunities for play does it include?

- What's the overall narrative of your design? What are the flows?

- Where do you anticipate kids will be using your site or app? What's the context in which they'll be using it?

- How and where will you market it?

Once you fully understand what it is you're designing, why you're designing it, and for whom, you can start your research and design process. If you're not going to be doing the actual visual design or coding yourself, find partners to help you with these aspects of the process early on, so they can lend their expertise at the outset and inform you about things like feasibility, time frame, and cost. There are quite a few sites available to help you find good people to work with on design and development; in the U.S., elance.com is a good resource, as is iFreelance.com. You can also check LinkedIn or other social networks for recommendations.

Next, the Design Particulars

In this next section, we'll address some of the design specifics you should consider as you begin the design process. These areas present some of the biggest challenges you'll face, so it's a good idea to spend a little more time attending to them. These areas include the following:

- Navigation and wayfinding

- Design patterns

- Data collection

- Community and social

- Advertising

Navigation and Wayfinding

- How will kids move and progress through your design?

- How will they get back to the starting point?

- How will they know where they are in the site or app at any given time?

- Do your navigation elements provide the right level of feedback at the right time?

- How will kids get help if they have questions?

- Do you have an area just for parents that's easily accessible from within the experience?

- What provisions have you made for exploration and discovery?

- Have you established a linear flow with opportunity for diversion?

Design Patterns

- Are you using consistent design techniques for navigation, fields, content, and layout that work for your target age group?

- Are you using color appropriately for your target age group?

- Will your users understand and be able to use the icons and symbols in your pattern library?

- How are you using audio? Do your audio cues move your users through the experience?

- How do all the elements of your design help kids understand how to use it? Is there anything extraneous that might be getting in the way?

- What can you do to simplify the experience and make it more seamless?

Data Collection

- Are you collecting any personal and identifiable information from children under 13? Why? How will you use it?

- Are any forms you've designed optimized for your users' reading, typing, and cognitive skills?

- Do your data collection mechanisms offer contextual help?

- Is the value proposition of your data collection efforts made clear in the experience? What will kids gain from giving you data?

- What provisions have you made for kids so they don't have to remember complex passwords or login information?

- Are you COPPA-compliant?

- Do you have information for parents to let them know why you're collecting this data?

- Do you have the proper parental opt-ins?

- Do you have an easy-to-understand privacy policy available from within the experience?

Community and Social

- Are kids able to communicate with each other within your environment? How?

- Will a moderator be available to solve problems or receive reports?

- Is this moderator reviewing all messages posted on the site before they appear, or can kids communicate on the fly?

- Are your rules for engagement clear, flexible, and easy to follow?

- Do you have free-form chat? If so, do you have the appropriate parental consent mechanism in place?

- What's your privacy policy? Where in the experience will it live?

- How will kids (or parents) report abusive behavior?

- Do you have the right mix of creating, saving, and sharing activities in your product, so kids don't focus entirely on communication?

Advertising

- Will your site have ads?

- Who will you allow to advertise within your product?

- Will the ads be targeted at kids or at their parents?

- If your ads target kids, how will you clearly differentiate advertising content from actual site content?

- Are you following CARU (Children's Advertising Review Unit) recommendations and best practices for ads?

- If you're designing an app, are any in-app purchases or ads compliant with platform guidelines?

- Do in-app purchases require a password or parental code?

- Do parents have the option to turn off in-app purchases or suggestions? If not, is it relatively difficult for kids to make in-app purchases without parental consent?

Finally, Getting It Out There

Once you have your site or app designed, coded, and fully tested, you're ready to put it out there for kids.

Here are some checklists to help with the logistics of launching your product.

Websites

If you are designing a site, you'll need to get a URL and a domain server to host your site. There are companies that can set up the URL and domain hosting for you, for a low monthly fee. These are generally easy to use and will walk you through the steps of uploading your site, establishing and directing it to your URL, monitoring your site, and making changes to content or designs.

Here's a quick checklist for launching your site. These are the basics. You can find a lot more information about this by taking Google's Webmaster Academy.[2]

- Have you checked your site for spelling, grammar, and copy errors? (There's nothing worse than launching a site only to find "lorem ipsum" content in there somewhere.)

- Have you selected a domain name that is short, easy to type, and easy to remember?

- Have you registered your domain name?

- Have you made hosting arrangements for your site?

- Have you tested your site on multiple browsers to make sure that it works across the board?

- If you've designed a responsive site, have you tested it on multiple devices?[3]

- Have you optimized your site for search engines?[4]

---

2 https://support.google.com/webmasters/answer/6001102

3 http://alistapart.com/article/responsive-web-design/

4 https://support.google.com/webmasters/answer/35291?hl=en

Games and Apps

If you've created an app, you'll want to think about the following before submitting it to a platform app store:

- Have you written a brief, compelling description of your app that provides basic information, including what your app does, who it's for, and what its goals are?

- Have you gathered several key screenshots to use for marketing purposes?

- Do you have a parent-friendly privacy policy ready that you can link to from the app description?

- Have you identified your app's relevant tags and keywords to ensure that your app will show up when users search for those terms?

- If your app is for international audiences, do you have all copy translated into the languages spoken in the countries you're targeting?

- Have you collected testimonials from your testers (both kids and parents) that you can use to market your app?

- Have you set up an informational site that you can direct people to?

TIP SUBMITTING TO AN APP STORE

Individual platforms have different rules and policies about submitting apps. You'll want to make sure that you're familiar with these rules before sending your app in for review. The good news is, the platforms have lots of information available, so you can make sure you're doing it right. Go to the sites listed here for detailed information about how to submit your product:

- **Apple iOS App Store Distribution:** https://developer.apple.com/support/appstore/

- **Google Play:** http://developer.android.com/distribute/index.html

- **Windows Store:** http://msdn.microsoft.com/en-us/library/windowsphone/

Designing for Kids...and Beyond

If you've made it this far, you've learned a great deal about what you need to know to design the next big site or app for kids. You've watched kids grow from tiny non-readers with limited motor and cognitive skills to complex pre-teens with sophisticated problem-solving and deductive reasoning skills. You understand how designing for a 6-year-old is different from designing for a 9-year-old, and why this is the case. And you're able to quickly identify some types of research activities to do with children of any age.

However, many of you won't find yourselves designing for kids anytime soon. Perhaps you're a designer at an agency, working on many different types of projects for diverse clients. Maybe you work in-house designing sites or apps for a financial service, ecommerce, or pharmaceutical company. Or perhaps you're not a designer at all, but involved in education, client services, sales, or management. My challenge to you is, how might you use some of this information in your current role? How could some knowledge of how to design for kids impact the way you work with people on a regular basis?

The desire to play never fully leaves us, no matter how much we "grow up." For example, my father, a brilliant man and respected physician, keeps "accidentally" deleting the operating system from his PC because he was "just playing around" and wanted to see what would happen. This desire to learn by doing, the need to immerse ourselves in something "fun," and the joy that comes from simply using our hands and our minds to make stuff happen, stays with us throughout our lives.

Submitting to the Apple iOS App Store

The Apple iOS App Store has a very strict process and set of rules you'll need to follow if you want to submit an app. If you skip any of the items requested or any of the steps in the process, you run the risk of getting your app rejected. Here are the basics:

1. In order to develop an iOS app, you'll need an Apple Developer account from the iOS Development Center. This account establishes your business within the app store so you can get paid if you charge for your app. You (or your developer) will need to install xcode to start programming the app.

2. Once your app is coded and complete, it's time to craft a description of your app, which is the actual copy that users will see when they access your app from the app store. This copy should be brief and include a little information about what your app is, whom it is for, and what the goals are. In short, its intent is to help users decide to download your app.

3. Next, pull a few screenshots from the app to give users a good idea of what it looks like, what it does, and how it works.

4. If your app is for kids, you'll want to include an online privacy policy that users can link to from the app description and the app itself. This will be primarily for a parent audience, so it should cover all the provisions your app makes for privacy and safety.

5. Next, identify your app's relevant tags and keywords to make sure that your app will show up in the app store search results when users search on those keywords.

6. You've already determined who your target audience is for the app, but there are some additional items you need to establish:

   - In which countries will your app be available? If you're pushing your app to stores for countries where English is not the first language, you'll need translated copy for the app description and keywords described earlier. If you'd like, you can submit different versions of the app descriptions within a single country, if you are targeting audiences with different language needs.

   - If you are making your app available to different markets with different languages, you'll need to include translated copy for all the content in the app itself.

7. Finally, determine which iOS versions will support your app and specify this information when submitting your app to the app store.

After you submit your app, it can take up to two weeks before you hear whether or not it was accepted. Make sure that you review all the App Store Review Guidelines to ensure that you're submitting it properly.

Companies with adult-oriented products are starting to incorporate some of the ideas presented in this book to engage their audiences. My favorite example of this is the extraordinary *Biblion Frankenstein* app, put out by the New York Public Library. It features literary criticism, commentary, and rare items from the library's collection—definitely not for kids—presented in a wholly immersive, self-guided experience. Using techniques like progression, achievement, exploration, and discovery, the app's creators tap into the innate need we all have to learn through play.

FIGURE 11.1
Biblion Frankenstein
uses principles for
designing for kids to
create a compelling
app for adults.

So go forth and design, for kids...*and* adults. I can't wait to see what you create.

INDEX

Buley, Leah
  The User Experience Team of One, 160

C

Caillou, 44–46
Candystand, 130–131
canned chat, 104–105
CARU (Children's Advertising Review Unit), 122
case study
  age 2-4 years, 65–66
  age 4-6 years, 84–85
  age 6-8 years, 108–109
  age 8-10 years, 137–139
  age 10-12 years, 156–157
Catapult Chaos, 118–119
cell phones, 150–151
challenge
  for age 4-6 years, 82–83
  designing for kids *versus* adults, 12–13
change, designing for kids *versus* adults, 14
chat
  anonymous, 153
  canned, 104–105
child-parent sessions, design research, 166
Children's Advertising Review Unit (CARU), 122
click sound type, 59
Club Penguin, 11, 99–100, 104
cognitive development learning concepts, 31–33
cognitive-control system, 14
collection of item activities, 93–94
color representation, 48–49
complexity elements, 120–122
concrete operational stage (Theory of Cognitive Development), 38–39
confirmation and error messages, 118–120
consent forms, 163–164
consistency, similarities between kids and adults, 15

constructionism concept, 125–126
container apps, 183
contextual inquiry, design research, 167–168
conversation, preoperational stage of cognitive development, 38
COPPA regulations, 104
Council on Communications and Media, 6–7

D

dangerous apps, 153
Daniel Tiger's Neighborhood, 52
data collection, 215
deductive reasoning, 144
demographic information collection, 130
design for kids *versus* adults, 12–14
Design of Everyday Things, The (Norman), 32
design process
  advertising, 216
  data collection, 215
  design patterns, 215
  general questions (why, who, and what), 212–214
  navigation and wayfinding, 214
  social communication, 216
design research
  with age 2-6 years, 165–168
  with age 6-8 years, 168–171
  with age 8-12 years, 172–174
  agenda, 162
  child-parent sessions, 166
  contextual inquiry, 167–168
  guidelines, 160–162
  informed consent, 163–164
  lab research, 168, 173
  master-apprentice model, 162
  one-on-one sessions, 172
  recruiting kids as participants, 165
  school setting observation, 172–173
  surveys, 174
diagramming, affinity, 22

K

kids
  designing for adults *versus*, 12–14
  similarities between adults and, 15–17
KiK Messenger, 153
Kingdom Rush, 143–145
Kuniavsky, Mike
  Observing the User Experience, 160

L

lab research, 168, 173
lagniappe, similarities between kids
  and adults, 16–17
launching websites, 217–218
learning
  as part of game, 75–78
  versus playing, 10–11
Lego-themed apps, 65–66
leveling up-type design, 88–90
Little Pim Spanish, 53–54
logic
  formal operations stage of cognitive
    development, 39
  inductive, 39
losing, as learning opportunity, 80
lying, idea of, 129–130

M

Machinarium, 144–146
master-apprentice model, 162
Minecraft, 120
Mini Sound Box, 59–61
Minifigures, 65–66
music, 59

N

navigation and wayfinding, design
  process, 214
Nick Jr., 55–56
Nickelodeon, 123–124
Norman, Don
  The Design of Everyday Things, 32

O

object permanence phase, 35
observational research
  participants, 18
  sample flowchart, 20–21
Observing the User Experience
  (Kuniavsky), 160
Omegle, 153
Online Ethics Center for Engineering
  and Science, 163
outside influences, 88–89
Ovemar, Emil (Toca Boca producer
  and cofounder), 67–69

P

Papert, Seymour (constructionism
  concept), 126
Parental Threshold for the Revolting
  (PTR), 25–26, 213
parents
  child-parent sessions, 166
  DIY parental consent, 132–133
  messaging controls, 51
  providing with usage tools and
    tips, 106
  upsell controls, 51
  volume controls, 51
participants
  for observational research, 18
  recruiting for design research, 165
PBS Kids Go!, 90
personal narrative and
  exploration, 146–149
Photo Grid-Collage Maker, 148–149
Piaget, Jean (Swiss psychologist)
  cognitive development learning
    concepts, 31–33
  Einstein on, 31
  intelligent test analysis, 30
  Theory of Cognitive Development, 31,
    34–40
  Three Mountain Test, 37

ACKNOWLEDGMENTS

First, a giant **thank you** to all the kids I've worked with over the years. Some of you are practically adults now, and will probably never know how much you've taught me. Extra special thanks go out to the kids who agreed to be interviewed for this book: Noah, Samantha, Andy, Iris, and Alexa.

To my parents, Barbara and Stephen Levin, and my-brother-doctor, Michael Levin, thanks for the unconditional love, support, laughter, and zany adventures. I wouldn't be where I am today if it weren't for you. All my love, always.

Much appreciation and love to my amazing extended family: Stephanie, Andy, Noah, Aunt Arlene, Uncle Barry, Aunt Lucille, Uncle Ed, Irene, Artie, Eric, Robin, Jill, Max, Ryan, Molly, Kami, Josh, Scott, Sherri.

Nicole Rittenhouse, your constant encouragement, faith, and check-ins helped keep me going and got me unstuck many times. Thanks for being there. To my gal pals who are like sisters: Benna Millrood, Melissa Rosenstrach Zimmerman, Jill Cohen Shaw, Lisa Kagel, Jennifer Blauvelt—I so appreciate your friendship and love.

A big thank you to the wonderful UX community, both local and global, for inspiring me, challenging me, and showing me new ways to look at the world. Special shout-outs to Michael Carvin, Kel Smith, Bryce Glass, Jeff Parks, Kevin Hoffman, John Ferrara, David Cooksey, Jeff Gothelf, Steve Portigal, Rachel Hinman, Indi Young, Lynne Polischiuk, Angela Colter, Livia Labate, Andrea Resmini, Adam Connor, Becca Deery, David Farkas, Russ Unger, Yoni Knoll, Will Sansbury, Boon Sheridan, John Yuda, Eduardo Ortiz, Chris Avore, Brad Nunnally, Aaron Irizarry, Marty Focazio, Wendy Green Stengel, Lori Cavallucci, Cennydd Bowles, Andrew Hinton, Chris Risdon, and Erin Cummings for the extra support and encouragement.

To my Refinery-Empathy Lab-Comcast-EPAM pals: Jon Ashley, Andrea Boff-Sutton, Kristin Dudley, Andrew Fegley, David Fiorito, Crystal Kubitsky, Kevin Labick, Ron Lankin, Tom Loder, Jonathan Lupo, Casey Malcolm, Bruce McMahon, Rob Philibert—thanks for 10+ years of love and laughter.

To all of you who helped make this book come alive: Emil Ovemar, Linnette Attai, Sabina Idler, and Catalina Naranjo-Bock for being great interviewees, reviewers, and consultants; Jason Cranford Teague, Stephen Anderson, and Allison Druin for the kind testimonials; and Brenda Laurel for the amazing foreword—my heartfelt thanks and appreciation.

Enormous gratitude to my editor, Marta Justak, for putting up with my liberal interpretation of deadlines and teaching me that writing is messy, imperfect, and non-linear.

Lou Rosenfeld, you're the reason this book came to fruition. Thanks for taking a chance on me. You're a leader and an inspiration.

Finally, Josh and Samantha, thanks for this crazy, wonderful, amazing life. I wouldn't have had the courage to go down this path if it weren't for you.

ABOUT THE AUTHOR

 **Debra Levin Gelman** is a writer, researcher, designer, and strategist in the field of interactive children's media. She has worked with clients including PBS Kids, Sprout, Scholastic, Crayola, NBC Universal, and Comcast to create sites, apps, and virtual worlds for kids. She led the research and design of *Planet Orange*—a financial-literacy site for elementary-school students, teachers, and parents—which won a USA Today Education "Best Bet" award.

Deb held a variety of agency and in-house positions before she landed in the Digital Strategy and Experience Design team at EPAM, where she currently serves as Director of User Experience. She speaks and leads workshops regularly at conferences including WebVisions, IA Summit, IxDA, UX Lisbon, and UXPA, and has written for *A List Apart* and *UX Magazine*.

Originally from the Philadelphia, PA area, Deb earned undergraduate degrees in Visual Media and Psychology from American University, and a masters in Information Design and Technology from The Georgia Institute of Technology. She returned to Philadelphia in 2000 where she lives, works, and plays with her amazing husband, Josh, and fabulous daughter, Samantha, who wants to be a princess paleontologist when she grows up.